EMPIRE OF THE INCAS

REVISED EDITION

GREAT EMPIRES OF THE PAST

GREAT EMPIRES OF THE PAST

EMPIRE OF THE INCAS

REVISED EDITION

BARBARA A. SOMERVILL

LUCY C. SALAZAR, HISTORICAL CONSULTANT

CHELSEA HOUSE
PUBLISHERS
An imprint of Infobase Publishing

Chelsea House
An imprint of Infobase Publishing
132 West 31st Street
New York NY 10001

Library of Congress Cataloging-in-Publication Data
Somervill, Barbara A.
  Empire of the Incas / Barbara A. Somervill. — Rev. ed.
    p. cm. — (Great empires of the past)
  Includes bibliographical references and index.
  ISBN 978-1-60413-158-1
  1. Incas—History. 2. Incas—Social life and customs. I. Title.
  F3429.S66 2009
  985'.019—dc22   2008045807

Chelsea House books are available at special discounts when purchased in bulk quantities for businesses, associations, institutions, or sales promotions. Please call our Special Sales Department in New York at (212) 967-8800 or (800) 322-8755.

You can find Chelsea House on the World Wide Web at http://www.chelseahouse.com

Text design by Annie O'Donnell
Cover design by Alicia Post
Produced by the Shoreline Publishing Group LLC
Editorial Director: James Buckley Jr.
Series Editor: Beth Adelman

Printed in the United States of America

Bang FOF 10 9 8 7 6 5 4 3 2 1

This book is printed on acid-free paper.

All links and Web addresses were checked and verified to be correct at the time of publication. Because of the dynamic nature of the Web, some addresses and links may have changed since publication and may no longer be valid.

CONTENTS

INTRODUCTION

UNCOVERING THE FACTS ABOUT THE INCA EMPIRE IS NOT easy. It takes experts of all kinds to understand the evidence the Inca left behind. Mathematicians work to unravel the only records left by people of the empire—*quipus*, which are knotted strings that counted the Inca people and what they produced down to the last dried potato. Archaeologists dig up ancient temples, buried cities, and mummies that tell of a complex society. Historians look into the writings of Spanish conquistadors (conquerors), priests, and government clerks—which are the only written records of the Inca culture.

All these experts must separate fact from fiction. The history of the Inca Empire is full of legends of stone warriors and visits from the gods, and not all of it really happened.

The work is made more difficult because the Inca had no written language or numerical system. The Inca civilization passed its history along by oral tradition—telling stories. So the founding of the empire may have taken place in 1200—or not. Dates and details of the early Inca Empire are all estimates.

The Spanish arrived in 1524. Because they loved to write about everything they saw and did, they were the ones who provided the first written records of Inca life. But before that, from 1200 to about 1525, we have a blend of fact and fiction, legends and daring deeds, mixed with cultural pride. Historians have been frustrated, because there is simply no way to separate stories of greatness from actual feats of greatness.

Even the term *Inca* can be confusing. The word *Inca* refers to a single person, a social class, and a civilization. *Inca* is a Quechua word

CONNECTIONS

What Are Connections?

Throughout this book, and all the books in the Great Empires of the Past series, there are Connections boxes. They point out ideas, inventions, art, food, customs, and more from this empire that are still part of the world today. Nations and cultures in remote history can seem far away from the present day, but these connections demonstrate how our everyday lives have been shaped by the peoples of the past.

that means "leader" or "chief." The empire's supreme leader, a kind of king or emperor, had the title Inca or Sapa Inca (unique leader or chief). Thirteen Sapa Incas ruled the empire throughout its history, and some were more successful than others. The last true Sapa Inca was Atahuallpa (r. 1532–1533). Although there were Sapa Incas after Atahuallpa, such as Manco Inca and Tupac Amaru, they had no power. Once the Spanish took over, they controlled the land and the people—and the Sapa Inca.

The Sapa Inca led a noble class of about 1,000 men. These nobles were called Incas or Capac Incas, and they served as government, religious, and military leaders of the empire. All were relatives of the Sapa Inca. Women played leadership roles in some areas of life, especially those that involved other women, but they were generally not leaders of groups that included men.

Today, people often refer to all citizens living under the rule of the Incas as "Incas"; they were not. They were conquered cultures and civilizations that became part of the Inca Empire. Inca subjects often continued to worship their own gods. This was allowed, as long as they also worshipped the main Inca gods: the sun, the moon, and thunder-lightning. They wore their ethnic style of clothing and actually were not allowed to wear the clothes or headgear of any other ethnic group or region.

The empire began in Cuzco. This village was founded by Manco Capac, the first Sapa Inca, and settled by his followers. The village still exists today in southeastern Peru. Eventually, Inca influence spread from the eastern foothills of the Andes Mountains to the Pacific Ocean, from present-day Ecuador in the north to modern Chile and Argentina in the south. The Sapa Inca ruled over land that stretched 2,500 miles along western South America, or roughly the distance from Los Angeles, California, to Charleston, South Carolina. But this is really just an estimated guess, because no records, detailed maps, or exact borders exist from those times.

The Inca Empire did not begin a completely new culture and civilization, developing unique ideas about religion, agriculture, arts, music, or warfare. Instead, it assimilated (took in and absorbed) other cultures. Conquered peoples inside the empire became part of its huge labor force and learned Inca values and beliefs.

The empire welcomed new ideas and, after experimentation, improved on the arts and technology of others. For example, the Inca Empire is noted for beautiful, complex, and durable buildings made of stone. This kind of building with stone is called masonry. The Inca did not invent advanced masonry techniques. However, they were inspired by the work of the conquered Tiahuanaco culture that lived near Lake Titicaca. The Incas improved upon and adapted these Tiahuanaco masonry techniques. Museum-quality gold and silver metalwork techniques were borrowed from artisans of the Chimu people of the Moche Valley, another earlier culture assimilated by the Incas.

The 13 Sapa Incas

There are no exact birth and death dates for these leaders, except for the deaths of the last five. Instead, these are the estimated dates of when they ruled.

Manco Capac, ruled ca. 1200
Sinchi Roca, ruled ca. 1228–1258
Lloque Yupanqui, ruled ca. 1258–1288
Mayta Capac, ruled ca. 1288–1318
Capac Yupanqui, ruled ca. 1318–1348
Inca Roca ruled, ca. 1348–1378
Yahuar Huacac, ruled ca. 1378–1408
Huiracocha, ruled ca. 1408–1438
Pachacuti (Cusi Yupanqui), ruled 1438–1471
Tupac Yupanqui, ruled 1471–1493
Huayna Capac, ruled 1493–1525
Huáscar, ruled 1525–1532
Atahuallpa, ruled 1532–1533

THE *CRONISTAS*

Much of what is know today about the Inca Empire comes from Spanish *cronistas*—soldiers, clerks, and priests who wrote detailed accounts of the history, customs, and daily lives of Inca citizens. Some (but not all) of the Spanish who came to the Inca Empire kept journals, wrote letters, and recorded the events of their conquest. *Cronistas* provide primary source material (history written by the people who lived it) from the viewpoint of a conquering people. The Spanish came from

This 18th-century painting shows the succession of Inca rulers, beginning with Manco Capac and ending with King Ferdinand VI of Spain.

a very different cultural background and did not always appreciate or understand the Inca.

Felipe Guaman Poma de Ayala (ca. 1538–ca. 1620), an Andes native, wrote the longest and perhaps most valuable document about the Inca Empire, *La nueva crónica y buen gobierno* (the new chronicle and good government). This 1,179-page manuscript contains descriptions of Inca culture, history, occupations, religious practices, and government. Guaman Poma included more than 400 drawings with his writing. Guaman Poma's manuscript was written in the early 1600s, but was not discovered until 1908, when German scholar Richard Pietschmann found it in the Royal Danish Library in Copenhagen.

Garcilaso de la Vega (1539–1616) was the son of the Spanish conquistador Sebastian de la Vega Vargas and the Inca princess Chimpu Ocllo. Garcilaso had a European-style education but he also knew and respected the Inca culture. His writings about the Inca civilization are detailed and present an exciting picture of the people and their lives. There are several volumes, all grouped under the title *The Incas: Royal Commentaries*. The Royal Council of Madrid was not enthusiastic about Garcilaso de la Vega's chronicle, so they changed the title from *Royal Commentaries* to *General History of Peru*.

Scholars know very little about Juan de Betanzos (ca. 1550), author of *Suma y narracíon de los Inca* (narrative of the Incas). He was Spanish by birth but lived in Peru most of his life. Betanzos may have been a Spanish scribe (a person who copies out documents) or a government clerk, as well as an interpreter who investigated native traditions and customs. He married an Inca woman, lived in Cuzco in the 1540s, and was fluent in Spanish and Quechua (the language of the Incas). The Spanish *corregidors* (royal administrators) certainly found his skills to be useful. His *Suma y narracíon* has been translated into English and provides one of the earliest accounts of Inca culture.

Cronista Pedro de Cieza de León (ca. 1518–1560) was born and educated in Spain and traveled through much of the Inca Empire as a soldier. His *Crónica del Peru* (chronicle of Peru), published in 1553, presents richly detailed accounts of the Spanish conquest from a military viewpoint. He provides accurate geographical descriptions of the region and explanations of the Inca government and culture. He also explains the military strategy used by the relatively small Spanish conquering forces in defeating the Incas.

Cieza de León observed the Inca people and had a deep understanding of their ways. This is how he described how hard the Inca work in his *Crónica*: "No one who was lazy or tried to live by the work of others was tolerated; everyone had to work. Thus on certain days each lord went to his lands and took the plow in hand and cultivated the earth, and did other things. Even the Incas themselves did this to set an example. And under their system, there was none such in all the kingdom, for, if he had his health, he worked and lacked for nothing; and if he was ill, he received what he needed from the storehouses."

Soldiers marveled at the technology and wealth of the Incas, but Roman Catholic priests saw only "pagan" (from a primitive religion) rites and "heathen" (not Christian) idols. The goal of the Catholic clergy in Peru was to convert the native people to Christianity. In their desire to stamp out Native worship, priests reduced Inca sacred idols and temples to rubble and replaced the Inca heritage with their own. The Spanish clergy had mixed success; the Native population hid the locations of many sacred Inca sites and religious treasures and mingled their traditional polytheism (worship of more than one god) with Roman Catholic practices.

Father Bernabé Cobo (1582–1657), a Jesuit priest and missionary (a person sent to a foreign country to promote a religion), wrote the least biased, most accurate account of Inca history by a priest in his book *Historia del Nuevo Mundo* (the history of the new world). He arrived in Peru in 1599, and traveled extensively throughout Peru and northern Bolivia. Cobo was an early historian. Most of his writings were based on library research using the work of earlier Spanish *cronistas*, as well as some personal observations and oral information. Still, Cobo compiled a large and relatively accurate catalog of the Inca Empire.

In addition to the Spanish accounts, a few Native Andeans wrote histories of the Incas. These chroniclers wrote much later than the Spanish. The best known of these was Juan de Santa Cruz Pachacuti Yamqui Salcamayhua, who wrote a history of Peru in the early 17th century. Another Native historian was Inca Diego del Castro Titu Cusi Yupanqui. Titu Cusi wrote 22 volumes on the history of the Incas and their conquest by the Spanish. Using both Spanish and Native American resources provides a balanced view of Inca history.

THE INCA LEGACY

The list of lessons to be learned from the Inca Empire is a long one. The civilization thrived even though it did not have a written language, a number system, or one of humanity's greatest inventions—the wheel.

Despite these obvious handicaps, the Inca Empire developed and administered a type of government in which it was rare to find a citizen who was hungry, naked, or homeless. Under Inca rule, the sick were generally well-cared for and the elderly could expect to receive tender consideration. All this occurred without corruption in a society that was relatively crime-free. No modern government has provided so completely for its citizens.

Although it is difficult for people to understand today, the Inca method of record keeping using strings and knots—the *quipu*—was as effective at keeping statistics as today's powerful computers. Every region, every farm, and every single taxpayer appeared in the *quipus*. The Incas accepted no errors in their records.

Inca building technology offers lessons many countries would find valuable today. Inca masons (craftsmen who practiced masonry) built walls of stone in which the face of the wall is designed to fit so tightly that the mortar (the cement that holds the stones together) is hidden.

These walls have held up over many centuries and countless earthquakes. Engineers built irrigation ditches, canals, and aqueducts (channels for carrying water) that provided fresh water and sanitation to cities at a time when European towns had open sewers that spread disease among the population.

CONNECTIONS

Who Speaks Quechua?

Some Quechua words have found their way into the English language. These include coca, condor, guano (bat or bird manure, used for fertilizer), lima (as in the bean), llama, puma, quinine, quinoa (a type of grain), and vicuña (an Andean animal that is related to the llama; the word also means the cloth made from the wool of that animal).

Paved roads ran up the Andes Mountains, along cliff edges, over deserts, and through jungles. Many of those roads still exist today. Bridges spanned wide gaps between the mountains that were hundreds of feet deep. They lasted more than 100 years, even though they were made of just reeds, leather, and logs. By 1500, the planned city of Cuzco had more than 4,000 stone buildings, complete with sparkling fountains, rock-lined sewers, and large public plazas.

The empire combined diverse cultures into one civilization ruled by a single man, the Sapa Inca. Throughout the realm, all citizens were required to learn Quechua, the language of the Incas. Subjects all followed the same laws and suffered the same punishments for illegal acts—which were surprisingly few, since the punishment for most crimes was death.

A network of administrators, record keepers, and government spies kept the government running smoothly. Corruption, jealousy, and ambition were not common among Inca leaders. From birth to death, most Inca subjects accepted their roles in life and the laws that governed them: Do not be lazy, steal, lie, cheat on your spouse, or murder. The Inca civilization thrived under a simple philosophy: Work hard, pay taxes, and want for nothing.

PART · I

HISTORY

THE BEGINNING OF THE EMPIRE

THE EMPIRE AT ITS GREATEST

THE FINAL YEARS OF INCA RULE

CHAPTER 1

THE BEGINNING OF THE EMPIRE

THERE ARE MANY LEGENDS ABOUT HOW THE FIRST SAPA Inca, Manco Capac, and his wife, Mama Ocllo, established the Inca Empire. The legends are imaginative, creative, and compelling. They also form the basis for the cultural history of the South American country known today as Peru.

One legend tells of four brothers: Ayar Cachi, Ayar Uchu, Ayar Auca, and Ayar Manco. Their family lived in the cavern of Pacaritambo, a deep cave cut into the Andes Mountains. The four brothers and their four sisters left their home in search of a better life. The first brother, Ayar Cachi, had mystical powers that made his brothers and sisters jealous. The brothers tricked Ayar Cachi into returning to their cave, then they blocked it with stones to prevent Ayar Cachi from escaping.

The remaining siblings continued on their journey. When they reached Mount Huanacauri, Ayar Uchu turned to stone and became a holy shrine, or *huaca*, revered by the Inca people. This left Ayar Auca and Ayar Manco, who walked to a small village where Ayar Auca became frightened and fled. He scrambled across the rough landscape until he was exhausted. Then he sat down to rest and, like his brother, he turned to stone.

Ayar Manco traveled on with his sisters, finally arriving at a place between the Urubamba and Apurímac Rivers. There, Ayar Manco founded the city of Cuzco and the culture that would later become the Incas. Manco selected his sister Mama Ocllo as his wife because she was pleasant and eager to please people. The marriage explains the Inca custom of a Sapa Inca usually marrying his sister.

OPPOSITE
Manco Capac, known as the "son of the sun," was the first ruler of the Incas. He is shown here in an 18th-century painting.

Ayar Manco changed his name to Manco Capac and declared himself ruler over the new society. Later, the title of Sapa Inca was most often passed to a son of the primary wife, the *coya*. (Sapa Incas could also have many other, secondary wives.) The crown did not always go to the firstborn son, but whichever son of the *coya* seemed best suited to become the emperor.

Mama Ocllo married her brother, Manco Capac, and together they ruled the earliest Inca Empire. She is shown in this 18th-century painting holding her traditional symbol, the moon.

Another version of the Inca Empire's beginning involves Manco Capac, Mama Ocllo, and the sun god, Inti. The tale began as members of 10 clans (clans, called *ayllus* in the Inca language, are a group of related families) followed Manco Capac on his journey. Along the way, the sun god gave Manco Capac a golden rod, commanding him to plunge the rod into the earth when Manco arrived at a place he thought would be suitable for a settlement. The story says Manco chose a high plain in the Andes Mountains. He stuck the rod in to the ground and it disappeared. That is where he and his community founded Cuzco. Manco Capac then built a temple, the Intihuasi, to honor the sun on the exact spot where the golden rod disappeared into the earth.

These legends have been passed down from father to son, mother to daughter. Historians accept that Manco Capac was the founding father and the first ruler of a clan of people who lived in the Andes. The city of Cuzco still stands today. But exact details of when and how the empire began remain a mystery.

Equally mysterious are the many civilizations that thrived in the Andes and the surrounding regions before the Incas came to power. These civilizations contribute to the Inca story because they contributed to the art, culture, political organization, and religious beliefs of the Inca Empire. The names given to these cultures are not necessarily what the people called themselves, because archaeologists name various cultures after the locations where ruins of their civilizations have been found. So, for example, the Moche culture was a group of people who once lived in the Moche Valley in northern Peru.

Pre-Columbian (before Christopher Columbus arrived in the Americas in 1492) civilizations are recognized as cultures or horizons. A culture is the beliefs, society, art, and lifestyle of a contained group. A horizon describes cultural beliefs, art, and lifestyles spread over a large region and a number of diverse ethnic groups.

The early cultures that most influenced the Incas include the Chavín horizon, and the Moche, Paracas, Nazca, and Tiahuanaco cultures. These groups existed before Manco Capac founded the Inca Empire, and their artifacts (the objects they made that have been found by archaeologists) and technology were evaluated and incorporated into the Inca culture. None of these cultures had a written language, so dates and details of each group have been estimated by examining their artifacts.

THE CHAVÍN HORIZON

From 900 to 200 B.C.E., the people of Chavín thrived in the eastern *cordillera* (mountain range) of the Andes in present-day Peru. They controlled trade between the Pacific Ocean and the Amazon River region because of their important location along well-traveled mountain passes. Chavín art, beliefs, and social customs spread throughout the Andes through human contact and llama caravans (groups of people traveling together, often traders) that were packed with Chavín pottery, cloth, and metalwork.

This culture believed that the human and animal worlds were closely linked, and that it was possible to move between them in myths (traditional stories, often with a magical element) and religious ceremonies. They made religious images with anthropomorphized animals (animals with human forms or personality), including eagles, falcons, and snakes. Cats posed as humans appear on ceramic drinking vessels, urns (tall, rounded vases), plates, and on murals (wall paintings) in temples.

The Chavín developed the use of llama and alpaca wool in weaving. They advanced the use of natural dyes and cloth painting, as well as hand-spinning yarn and weaving on special looms that were braced against the weaver's back. These techniques became standard among the Chavín and were spread by traders among other cultures. By the time the Inca Empire began, Chavín weaving techniques were considered to produce the finest cloth.

CONNECTIONS

The Dig at Chavín de Huántar

The archaeological dig at Chavín de Huántar (located in the Andes Mountains in present-day Peru) has uncovered hundreds of artifacts and human remains. Among the most fascinating finds are 20 conch shell trumpets, carved and beautifully decorated. The Chavín trumpets are estimated to be between 2,500 and 3,000 years old.

At a modern press conference, a dozen musicians gathered to play conch shell trumpets. Conch trumpets create the deep, echoing tones heard in Andes traditional music today. They are also traditional instruments in Hawaiian, Japanese, and Polynesian music. Listen to music from the bands Inti-Illimani, Inkuyo, or Uakti to hear the sounds of instruments that were played as early as 3,000 years ago.

THE PARACAS CULTURE

Most of what is known today about the Paracas culture, which began in about 600 B.C.E., comes from studying a Paracas cemetery in southern Peru, near the city of Ica.

The bodies in the cemetery were wrapped in cloth and placed in large baskets in a crouching position. Many bodies were wrapped in finely embroidered cotton or wool, with designs of mythical creatures, animals, and geometric patterns.

Because the air is very dry, the bodies were naturally preserved as mummies. The condition of each mummified body tells much about the culture. For example, their skulls were flattened. Many Native American cultures considered a flat skull to be a sign of beauty, so they tied a board to the top of infants' heads at birth. The Paracas skulls give anthropologists (people who study human societies) an insight into the cultural beliefs of the Paracas people.

Along with the bodies, archaeologists found weapons, gold jewelry and ornaments, feather fans, the bodies of animals, pottery, and gourds. The artifacts provide information about the burial practices, technology, and art of the Paracas. Scientists know that the Paracas had technology for making cloth, metalwork, and ceramics. Because people were buried with many personal items, they assume that the culture believed in a life after death in which the dead would need weapons, food, and other things.

THE NAZCA CULTURE

Around 200 C.E., the Paracas culture gave way to the Nazca civilization. The Nazca people were artists and craftspeople who produced highly polished, decorated ceramics, and embroidered complex designs into wool and cotton cloth. The Nazca people also created remarkable rock patterns on the sandy desert soil. These patterns are so huge that they can only be seen from the air. The stone patterns represent birds, crabs, and flowers. One bird measures 400 feet by 300 feet. The edges of the designs point directly north, south, east, and west.

One of the culture's most remarkable skills was weaving. As with the Chavín, Nazca textile technology was passed from mother to daughter over many generations. By the time the Inca Empire emerged, the textile technology of both

This Nazca image of a monkey is traced in the sandy desert soil of Peru. It is so big that it is visible only from the air.

Fly With the Nazca?

The Nazca are a people who date back to around 200 C.E. and who lived in what is today known as southern Peru. A Nazca legend tells of Antarqui, a boy who helped the Incas during battles by flying overhead and reporting on enemy soldiers and their locations. Nazca ceramic artifacts (the objects they made that have been found by archeologists), portray flying people. In addition, cloth has been found in Nazca tombs that has such a tight weave that it could hold air. When tested by a hot air balloon manufacturer, the cloth was shown to have a tighter weave than the cloth that company used for making modern hot air balloons. Could the Nazca possibly have had the technology to fly?

Peter James and Nick Thorpe, in their book *Ancient Inventions,* suggest they may have, based on an archaeological experiment done by the Explorers Society. They write on page 110:

The Society tested the feasibility [possibility] of Nazca ballooning by construction of their own balloon, which they named Condor I. It was made from cotton and wood, with a gondola of reeds from Lake Titicaca to hold the passengers. The balloon was to be filled with hot smoke produced from burning extremely dry wood. . . .

On November 23, 1975, American Jim Woodman of the Explorers Society and English balloonist Julian Nott ascended to 380 feet in Condor I, stayed in the air for several minutes and then descended again safely, thus completing a remarkable piece of experimental archaeology. Of course this does not prove that the ancient Nazcans did fly, but it certainly shows that it is a very real possibility.

early cultures had deeply influenced the practices of spinning, dyeing, and weaving throughout the Andes.

THE MOCHE CULTURE

In the Moche and Chicama valleys of Peru, a civilization emerged that lasted roughly 600 years. They are called the Moche culture, a clan that thrived from about 100 to 700. The Moche developed a dominant class of noblemen that included priests and military leaders. They founded the first kingdom of the Andes and united weaker cultures under their king.

Like other early civilizations in the Americas, the Moche had no written language. However, archaeologists have discovered much about the Moche people's beliefs and practices by examining their ceramics. Pictures on bowls, jars, urns, and plates portray the Moche people in every aspect of life. Moche doctors perform brain surgery and set broken bones. Weavers spin and work their looms. Messengers carry important news along Moche roads while ancient soldiers use their slingshots and lances (weapons with a hard point mounted on a wooden pole) to protect their kingdom. Moche pottery also shows pictures of food, boats, houses, and farming practices, along with common animals such as llamas, pumas, frogs, and birds.

Moche construction methods were advanced for their time. The culture produced many large buildings, usually made of adobe (bricks made of straw and mud and dried in the sun). At Cerro Blanco in Peru, pyramids stand as a reminder of the Moche culture. The Huaca del Sol (Shrine of the Sun) and the Huaca de la Luna (Shrine of the Moon) were massive temples made of adobe blocks and built on huge temple platforms. The Huaca de la Luna's base measures 750 feet by 450 feet.

These pyramids existed when the Incas conquered the people living in the Moche Valley. That was about 600 years after the Moche civilization had disappeared. The ability to make adobe bricks that lasted must have impressed Inca architects. Although later Inca architecture used cut stone, early public buildings and houses for farmers in some regions used adobe bricks.

Because the Moche Valley is in the dry desert of northern Peru, it was not easy to grow food. The Moche developed advanced agricultural techniques to overcome this problem. They used guano (sea bird droppings) and livestock manure to fertilize their fields, and they built aqueducts to carry water for irrigation (bringing water to the fields to help crops grow) and for human use. These techniques were still in use when the Inca Empire began. The Incas were quick to recognize that Moche agricultural technology enabled them to grow more food. The use of irrigation and fertilizers reached its height during Inca days, but the original idea came from the Moche.

THE TIAHUANACO CULTURE

The Tiahuanaco civilization thrived on the southern shore of Lake Titicaca, in present-day Bolivia. Dates for the Tiahuanaco vary; some

The Oldest Observatory

In 2006, archaeologists working in the Andes discovered the oldest observatory found in the Americas. The site dates back before Inca times. It is a 4,200-year-old stone building that was used to mark the winter and summer solstice (when the sun is at its lowest and highest points in the sky).

The observatory was built on top of a pyramid. It was positioned in such a way that it could be used to decide when to plant and harvest crops.

In addition to the observatory, archaeologists also found clay sculptures and a mural (wall painting). The site, called Ventarrón, was found in the heart of Moche country, in the Moche and Chicama Valleys of Peru, but it is hundreds of years older than the Moche culture. The mural, the oldest so far found in the Americas, shows a deer caught in a net.

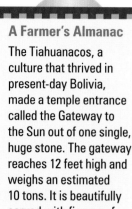

archaeologists believe the Tiahuanaco culture began in 100, and others think it was closer to 200. The dates when they disappeared also vary. Estimates range from 600 to 1250, with 1150 being the most likely time.

This was a culture of architects (people who design buildings), masons (people who work with stone or brick), and advanced building technology. No early South American cultures developed the wheel, yet these ancient people built massive stone temples, courts, and cities. The Tiahuanaco developed masonry to such a high degree that they could build large stone buildings where the blocks fit together so well that the mortar, or cement, between them is almost invisible. They carved stones to fit one inside the next using copper clamps and tenons (carved joints).

By the time the Incas met the Tiahuanacos, their civilization had collapsed. But they still were master builders, and the Inca absorbed their technology. Before the Incas met the Tiahuanacos, the Incas did build stone buildings. But the Inca buildings were not very grand. The master masons brought from Lake Titicaca helped improve the quality of Inca stonework.

THE FIRST INCAS

The Inca Empire began with a small group of people who lived in crude homes and scrambled for food. They spent their earliest years defending their territory from invading enemy tribes and trying to grow enough crops to feed themselves through droughts and famines. The first eight Inca rulers focused all their attention on Cuzco and its surrounding towns. In the early days, the Inca population was well under 10,000 people, and Cuzco under Manco Capac probably had only 500 residents.

In the early history of the Incas, it is difficult to separate the myths from the facts. Retelling this history is made even more difficult because the Incas had no written language, and oral history—remembering history by telling stories—can sometimes change as the story is told over and over. Still, there is a story of how the Inca civilization began.

The first Inca ruler, Manco Capac, and his wife (and sister), Mama Ocllo, brought together the small tribes living near Cuzco. The tribes formed *ayllus* (clans) under Manco Capac's guidance. The *ayllu* system lasted through the 300 years of the Inca Empire.

The new city demanded constant attention to make sure the people had the basic elements of life: food and water, clothing, and shelter. The Incas had to build housing, plant crops, hunt, and find safe drinking water. Manco Capac also built a sun temple, Intihuasi, so that the people of Cuzco could honor their main god.

Blending the four tribes around Cuzco was not difficult. The members of these tribes were farmers who had no interest in war. However, neighboring tribes were not as friendly. A significant achievement of Manco Capac's reign was to provide a safe, secure home for his people and an heir to provide continuous leadership.

After his death, Manco Capac's son and heir, Sinchi Roca, ruled from roughly 1228 to 1258. Among Sinchi Roca's first duties was to build a palace for himself and his family, servants, and guards. The mummy of each Inca ruler remained in his original palace, along with his family and his servants, so each new Inca chief had to build a new palace.

In addition to building a new palace, improvements needed to be made to the Intihuasi temple, since the original, according to Spanish priest Bernabé Cobo, was "of humble and coarse adobe walls . . . because in those rustic times the people did not have a way to work stone as their descendants did later." The Intihuasi served two purposes for the Incas, providing a place to worship and intimidating people of neighboring tribes, who were amazed by the size of the temple. This was particularly true of civilizations that had no formal places to worship.

Cuzco's location high in the Andes Mountains had a short season for growing food and a long winter. The population needed more food, and it was the Inca ruler's responsibility to make sure they got it. Sinchi Roca had two ideas about how to make more farmland. The first was to build agricultural terraces along the sides of the mountains. The Inca used rocks to create terrace steps along the hillsides, and then filled these steps with soil. Humans and llamas carried millions of stones to form the terrace steps. Filling the terraces required thousands of baskets of soil, which then needed to be raked, planted, weeded, and watered.

Sinchi Roca's other idea was draining the local marsh. The project was even more difficult than building the terraces. Long, sloped channels to drain the water had to be cut into the earth using primitive tools.

CONNECTIONS

Open Markets Endure

The open markets established by Lloque Yupanqui, the third Inca ruler, were much like farmers' markets of today. Farmers brought crops, such as potatoes, corn, and quinoa (a type of grain) to trade with other vendors who offered cloth, leather goods, pottery, and dried and smoked meat or fish. The Incas did not have any currency, so all purchases were traded for other goods, based on values set by the buyer and seller. Three such markets existed in Cuzco, and the tradition continues to this day.

Today, market day in Andes Mountain towns brings a flurry of activity, as vendors set up stalls and buyers compare produce and goods being offered. Many of the products remain the same: woven cloth, leather goods, dried meat or fish, corn, potatoes, medicinal and cooking herbs, and pottery. Buyers can make purchases in cash now, but they can still swap cloth for fish, fish for pots, or pots for potatoes, too.

Buyers and sellers crowd a traditional open-air market in Chinchero, Peru.

Both these projects meant that Sinchi Rocha's son, Lloque Yupanqui, the third Inca chief, did not face additional agricultural demands. Instead, his main accomplishments, in addition to building himself a palace, included increasing the size and style of the Intihuasi, creating public markets, building roads, beginning to establish the Inca administrative system, and building the Acllahuasi.

The Acllahuasi was the home of the *acllas*, holy or chosen women. It became known as a center of fine weaving, and the cloth produced there was used in religious rites, to dress priests and nuns, and for the Inca chief's family. The women also made beer and served as priestesses for religious rites. Since the chosen women were well trained and among the most beautiful women of the empire, many became secondary wives for Inca nobles.

As the population grew, Cuzco expanded and much of the population moved farther from the center of town. Lloque Yupanqui realized that a better means of travel was essential and ordered roads to be built between the suburbs and the center of Cuzco. With better travel, the Inca chief and his administrators could continue to keep closer watch on citizens living at the edge of the empire.

Lloque Yupanqui began the Inca civil service system to help him take care of his subjects. He appointed *curacas* (men who were professional government employees) to assign work, collect taxes, and oversee government projects such as building roads and irrigation systems. The *curacas* became the foundation of the extensive Inca program to keep track of everything that happened in the empire.

The occupation of *curaca*, like all occupations under the Incas, was hereditary—passed from father to son. No one was allowed to change careers.

Once the roads were built and the *curacas* were appointed, Lloque Yupanqui went on an inspection tour. He believed that a good ruler personally observed how his citizens lived and his administrators worked. Future Inca chiefs followed his example, taking a hands-on approach to governing.

Lloque Yupanqui passed on his spirit and vision to his heir, Mayta Capac (r. ca. 1288–1318). This new ruler established a school system among Inca nobility, encouraged religious tolerance, and conquered the people of Tiahuanaco. Early in his reign, Mayta Capac decided that princes needed to learn about government and warfare. The schools he founded offered a limited curriculum that ensured future rulers would be prepared for leadership and government administrators would understand the general workings of the Inca civil service. The school concept expanded to include sons of the Inca chief's relatives, *curacas*, and of rulers whose tribes or clans had been absorbed into the Inca Empire.

At a time when some European rulers forced their subjects to follow the king's religion or suffer terrible consequences, Mayta Capac realized that different cultures honored their gods with the same reverence as the Incas felt toward their own gods. He wanted conquered people to worship the Inca gods, but he also allowed them to follow their personal beliefs.

Mayta Capac recognized the importance of skilled warriors, since the Inca Empire spent a fair amount of time protecting itself from invasion and expanding its territory by conquering others. During his reign, about one-fifth of the population served in the military, although this was not a large number of men. The empire's population was about 1,000 people, so Mayta Capac's army numbered about 200. To increase the efficiency of the military in moving from place to place, Mayta Capac improved roads to all the outer regions of the empire.

Mayta Capac's greatest contribution to the Inca Empire was conquering the Tiahuanacos, a culture of superb architects and masons. The Incas learned and adapted Tiahuanaco skills of stone cutting, shaping, and building, and applied that knowledge to making stronger and more beautiful stone buildings.

Some people were born to greatness, and others achieve greatness by their good looks. That was the case with Capac Yupanqui, who at first was not the heir to Mayta Capac. Unfortunately, the man who was his heir was too ugly to be the ruler. The Inca chief was believed to be the son of the sun, and how could a truly unattractive person represent the sun god? The people decided that Capac Yupanqui made a better-looking king, and his ugly brother disappeared from politics.

Weaving is still important in the Andes. This Quechua woman works on a loom to create traditional designs.

Capac Yupanqui looked westward toward the Pacific Ocean to expand his empire. There were many cultures along the coast, including powerful warrior states and clans of artisans and craftspeople. Capac Yupanqui prepared his army to move from the higher, colder, wetter Andes to fight on the lower, hotter, dryer coast. Then, culture by culture, he continued his plan of expansion by conquest. Some cultures were happy to join the Inca Empire, while others fought against the Inca army—and lost. Within a few weeks, Capac Yupanqui had conquered the coastal region and brought nearly 120,000 square miles of territory under his rule.

Under Capac Yupanqui, the Intihuasi and Acllahuasi became temples of solid stone. Cuzco expanded, as it had since the days of Manco Capac, with groves of trees, gardens, public plazas, and recreational areas. His *coya*, Cusi Hilpay, took an interest in the environment and had forests and gardens planted throughout the empire. Equally important, Capac Yupanqui recognized the growing need for fresh water. He promoted a variety of water projects, including bridges, aqueducts, canals, drains, and sewer lines.

While the empire flourished under Capac Yupanqui, his household was filled with intrigue and scheming driven by ambition. Capac Yupanqui had many wives. Normally, the future ruler would be chosen from the sons of the *coya*, the primary wife, in this case Cusi Hilpay. However, there was jealousy among the wives. Cusi Chimbo wanted her favorite son to be the next ruler. Cusi Hilpay's father was *curaca* of Anta, a powerful and influential region. Cusi Chimbo, a secondary

IN THEIR OWN WORDS

Amazing Builders

When the Spanish arrived in Peru, they were amazed by the skill of Inca builders. According to the Spanish priest Bernabé Cobo:

What amazes us the most when we look at these buildings is to wonder with what tools and apparatus could they take these stones out of the rocks in the quarries, work them, and put them where they are without implements made of iron, nor machines with wheels, nor using either the ruler, the square, or the plumb bob, nor any of the other kinds of equipment and implements that our artisans use.

To give credit where it is due, the Incas learned these skills from an older civilization, the Tiahuanacos. It was the Tiahuanacos who developed the skill of putting two stones together so tightly that a person could not slide a knife between the rocks. The Incas simply had the good sense to borrow quality technology and the boldness to claim that technology as their own.

(Source: Cobo, Father Bernabé. *The History of the New World*. Translated by Roland Hamilton. Austin, Tex.: University of Texas Press, 1983.)

wife, was jealous of Cusi Hilpay and arranged for Hilpay's son Quispe Yupanqui, who was direct heir to the throne, to be murdered. Capac Yupanqui disappeared at about the same time, and most historians believe he, too, was murdered. Cusi Chimbo's supporters named her son Inca Roca the new ruler.

Inca Roca did not want to suffer the same fate as his father and half-brother. Immediately after taking power, he married Cusi Chimbo, his mother and partner in the murder of his father and half brother. This way, one of her children would certainly be the next heir and she would not be tempted to murder him, too.

Inca Roca was the most productive of the early Inca chiefs and the first ruler to use the title "Inca." He chose to be called the Sapa Inca, which means "unique chief."

Inca Roca was interested in road building, city planning, architecture, and improving water works in the Inca Empire. One of his first efforts was the total reorganization of the Inca political and social structure. He divided the government administration into two sections: upper and lower segments, with all political, military, and social matters falling under his direct authority. He named many people from his own family line to government and social positions. Only the priests of the Intihuasi were still direct descendants of Manco Capac.

Inca Roca finished draining the marshes, a project begun by Sinchi Roca more than 100 years before. He ordered canals to be built to provide plenty of fresh water to two city districts. In addition, he built a reservoir to store fresh water for homes and to irrigate crops. This increased the number of fields that could be farmed.

Roads continued to be a major Inca undertaking. The Incas had only two means of transportation: by foot or by litter (a small carriage carried by several men). Since only Inca nobles and *curacas* were allowed to ride by litter, almost everyone walked. Llamas were used as pack animals to carry loads, but were too small to take humans, since they can only carry about 100 pounds.

Inca Roca's successor, Yahuar Huacac, had none of his father's ambition, vision, or productivity. Instead, he preferred to remain in his palace and enjoy a very dull and uneventful reign as Sapa Inca. According to legend, Yahuar Huacac was kidnapped when he was eight years old, and this event psychologically damaged him for life. He was so ineffective that he did not even arrange the building of his own palace.

One Spanish historian, Garcilaso de la Vega, claimed that Yahuar Huacac managed to raise an army of nearly 20,000 men, but de la Vega's claim is an exaggeration. The population of Cuzco at the time was roughly 4,200 people, including many women, children, and men too old to fight. Yahuar Huacac could count possibly 1,000 men suitable for military service. Even adding recruits from neighboring towns and conquered people, the largest army possible would be about 2,500 soldiers. It did not matter anyway, since Yahuar Huacac's army did not fight, conquer, or advance the empire.

Yahuar Huacac's heir, Huiracocha, was the eighth Sapa Inca and is remembered as the most cowardly. Huiracocha's approach to expanding the empire was to conquer and absorb other cultures—as long as the expansion was not too dangerous or too difficult. In many past situations, the victorious Inca army looted the conquered villages, killed civilians, and acted recklessly. Huiracocha did not want to lose the wealth held in conquered towns. He scooped up smaller cultures and incorporated them under his authority, keeping their wealth and using their labor force.

One legend claims that after a long military campaign, Huiracocha and his son Urco Inca, his heir, took a vacation in the mountains. The Chanca people chose this time to attack the Inca Empire. Huiracocha felt that he could no longer rule and gave up his throne to Urco Inca, who was not able to defeat the Chancas. Another tale says that facing the attack of the Chanca, father and son both fled out of cowardice.

They left the protection of Cuzco to a younger son of Huiracocha, Cusi Yupanqui. Cusi Yupanqui not only defeated the Chanca, but he went on to become the greatest of the Inca rulers, a true Sapa Inca.

CHAPTER 2

THE EMPIRE AT ITS GREATEST

THE STORY OF HOW CUSI YUPANQUI BECAME THE military leader of the Inca army, defeated the Chanca, and claimed the title Sapa Inca actually began with a vision. According to the writings of Spanish priest Bernabé Cobo, the sun god Inti spoke to young Cusi Yupanqui, saying, "Come here, my child, have no fear, for I am your father the sun. I know that you will subjugate [conquer] many nations and take great care to honor me and remember me in your sacrifices."

The sun god then presented images of the lands and people Cusi Yupanqui would conquer. Cusi Yupanqui lived in a time and culture where such visions were taken seriously. As events unfolded, he was able to turn his vision into reality.

According to the *cronistas* (soldiers, clerks, and priests who wrote detailed accounts of the history, customs, and daily lives of Inca citizens), the legend began as follows: In 1438, Cuzco came under attack from the Chancas, a violent, warlike culture much feared by the Incas. To escape capture and possible torture, the Sapa Inca, Huiracocha, and his son and heir, Urco Inca, fled to a stronghold in the Andes Mountains. This left younger son Cusi Yupanqui to defend the empire.

At this point, fact and fiction mingle. As the Chancas prepared their attack, Cusi Yupanqui dressed in the skins of a puma (an animal the Inca revered for its strength and cunning). Cusi Yupanqui led his soldiers against the Chanca and, as the legend goes, the sun god Inti caused the stones on the battlefield to rise as warriors and assist Cusi Yupanqui in defeating the dreaded Chancas.

OPPOSITE
Some of the steep streets in Cuzco, Peru, are lined with giant stones taken from ancient Inca palaces.

The young warrior saved Cuzco from defeat, then forced his father to step down as ruler. After casting aside his cowardly brother, Cusi Yupanqui declared himself Sapa Inca. From that time on he was called Pachacuti—the earthshaker.

INCA MILITARY MIGHT

One of Pachacuti's first projects was a military campaign to expand the empire. He had inherited a well-disciplined and experienced army. Every adult male between ages 25 to 50 had military training, and part of the ritual of manhood included getting weapons of war as gifts and learning how to use them. A well-equipped warrior wore padded cloth armor and a helmet, and carried a spear, a mace (a heavy club with a metal head studded with spikes), a slingshot, and a shield.

The military was organized in a similar way to a modern army. The Incas based their military structure on units of 10. A troop of 10 men had a troop leader, like today's corporal. Five troops of 10 had an officer similar to a sergeant, and units increased accordingly.

Officers oversaw groups of 100, 500, 1,000, 5,000, and 10,000 warriors. The Sapa Inca was commander in chief of the army, just as the president of the United States is today. Although most officers were appointed nobles, the military was one area in which commoners could rise through the ranks. An outstanding warrior was rewarded, regardless of his position in society.

The Incas recognized the value of a continuous chain of supplies for military operations. Roads stretched to the edges of the Inca Empire, and along the roads were storehouses from which the soldiers were fed, clothed, and armed. In addition, llamas followed the army in caravans, carrying additional supplies the warriors might need.

Military strategy was simple: The Inca forces were divided into three groups. The first group attacked from the front while the other two groups circled to attack the rear flanks (sides). If the enemy retreated to a fortress, the Incas cut off all their water, food supplies, and communications—a military strategy called "laying siege."

According to Albert Marrin in his book *Inca and Spaniard: Pizarro and the Conquest of Peru*, "The Inca approached the enemy in mass formations thousands strong. As they came within earshot, they set up an earsplitting racket; noise boosted their own courage and made the enemy jittery. Warriors blew conch-shell trumpets and bone whistles. They shook gourd rattles and beat drums covered with human skin. Men danced wildly, whirling, jumping, shouting. They boasted of their courage and jeered at the enemy as cowards. Some units bellowed this bloodcurdling chant:

> *We'll drink* chicha [beer] *from your skull*
> *From your teeth we'll make a necklace*
> *From your bones, flutes*
> *From your skin we'll make a drum*
> *And then we'll dance.*

Many enemies gave up before the fighting had even begun.

In battle, the Inca army lined up according to which weapon they carried. The first row were skilled with the slingshot and attacked opponents by throwing their smooth stones. Then came the common warriors with spears, and stone or metal clubs, and nobles armed with sharp battleaxes made of copper.

As new cultures were conquered, the Incas added the weapons of those cultures to their army. Bolas (ropes with three stones attached) were one such addition. When the bolas were spun around, then hurled, the stones encircled the arms or legs of an enemy, literally tying him up. Another welcome addition was the bow and arrow. The Incas had no archery skills, but their subjects from the Amazon region achieved such great accuracy with bows and arrows that they could shoot birds in flight.

As Sapa Inca and commander in chief of the military, Pachacuti declared that destruction in conquest was unacceptable. He prohibited his soldiers from destroying towns, massacring the enemy, or burning crops. Instead, as he took over an area, Pachacuti enlarged the Inca labor force with farmers, soldiers, artisans, and experienced leaders.

The ruler Pachacuti (r. 1438–1471) expanded the role of the Sapa Inca and brought a new sense of organization to continuing Incan conquests.

Defeated cultures that declared loyalty to Pachacuti were immediately integrated into the Inca civil system. Those who remained hostile met a brutal fate: Their skulls became drinking vessels, their skins were stretched over military drums, and their bones were carved into flutes.

The Sapa Inca approached every conquest by extending a hand of friendship and offering a caravan laden with gifts. His open diplomacy encouraged acceptance of Inca rule while reducing the costs in lives and supplies consumed by major battles. Pachacuti offered gifts of gold and cloth, and guaranteed peace to those who swore their loyalty to the Inca Empire. Not surprisingly, less powerful cultures chose to join the empire rather than die.

In 1463, Pachacuti decided to concentrate on administering his now vast empire. He named his son, Tupac Yupanqui, as the new commander in chief of the military. For more than four decades, father, son, and grandson, Huayna Capac, enlarged the Inca Empire until it stretched roughly 3,400 miles north to south along the Andes. The Incas controlled all the land from the Pacific Ocean to the eastern foothills of the Andes and the Amazon rainforest.

Pachacuti was a dictator, but he was also a caring ruler. He understood the need for defeated people to keep their dignity and heritage intact, because otherwise they would become rebellious. He appreciated certain basic needs of people—food, clothing, and shelter—and the civil administration of Pachacuti's reign made sure all citizens had these basics.

However, Pachacuti was not simply an idealist. Many of his ideas about government came from his understanding of how a ruler maintains control over a great number of conquered people. One way to avoid rebellion was by bringing a conquered culture's principal idols (images of their gods) to the Coricancha, the central temple in Cuzco, which replaced the Intihuasi.

Pachacuti claimed he honored these gods, and in fact, the Incas occasionally accepted new gods into their own beliefs. However, moving the idols of these gods to Cuzco was a symbol that the defeated culture's beliefs were captive. In war, armies brought idols of their primary gods into battle as a safeguard against the enemy. These idols were not merely images, but were believed to have the power of the god they represented. Thus, an army automatically lost the battle when its idol was captured. Once Pachacuti held a culture's idols in Cuzco, its

A New Golden Temple

The Coricancha replaced the Intihuasi in Cuzco as the Incas' principal house of worship. The Intihuasi was made from adobe—bricks of straw and mud dried in the sun. It was replaced by the stronger stone Coricancha under Capac Yupanqui, the fifth ruler of the Incas. The foundations of this newer stone structure are still in existence. The name *Coricancha* means the "place of gold," and this temple certainly was. The walls and ceilings were lined with golden plaques, plates, and statues. The representation of the main god, the sun god Inti, was a human face surrounded by many rays of light, all presented in shining gold.

people would not dare rebel, because Pachacuti would order the idols to be destroyed.

In the same way, Pachacuti ensured loyalty among the leaders of a conquered culture by providing the leaders' sons with an education. The former leaders continued to govern their people while their sons went to Cuzco to study and learn Inca customs. Education ensured an excellent future for the heirs, and also made sure they came to value Inca culture. The sons were also hostages of Pachacuti, who would not have hesitated to execute them if their fathers rebelled.

THE LAND OF THE FOUR QUARTERS

As the empire expanded, the land that came under the Sapa Inca's rule came to be called the Land of the Four Quarters, or Tahuantinsuyu. The quarters—Chichaysuyu (north), Antisuyu (east), Collasuyu (south), and Cuntisuyu (west)—were distinctly different in region, climate, earlier civilizations, and agriculture. At the heart of the empire stood Cuzco, the capital of the government and the religion. In the land of the Incas, all roads led to Cuzco.

On a modern map of South America, Tahuantinsuyu would include Ecuador and the southern section of Colombia, portions of Bolivia, Argentina, and Chile, and most of Peru.

Each quarter had its own capital, style of dress, crops, languages, art forms, and religious beliefs. Yet all followed the laws and cultural patterns of Inca life. Each region had government administrators to assign work, enforce the peace, collect taxes, and oversee the welfare of the people.

Each quarter was under the guidance of an *apu*, or regional head. Below the *apus* were several layers of *curacas* (men who oversaw large groups of households). The Inca Empire based its rule on units of 10, so every group of 10 households had a leader. Groups of 50 households reported to a more important foreman, and so on up the line. Prefects (chief officers) watched over increasingly larger groups: 100, 500, 1,000, 5,000, and 10,000 households.

As the empire grew, Pachacuti realized that he did not have enough Capac Incas (nobles who were directly descended from Manco Capac, the founder of the Inca Empire) to administer his government. To fill in the gaps, Pachacuti began a new level of nobles—Hahua Incas, who were nobles appointed to their rank by the Sapa Inca. Men who had served the Sapa Inca well, leaders from conquered cultures, and military officers could be appointed to the noble rank of Hahua Inca.

The Inca Empire changed its borders under various Sapa Incas, but always had its heart in the Andes Mountains of South America.

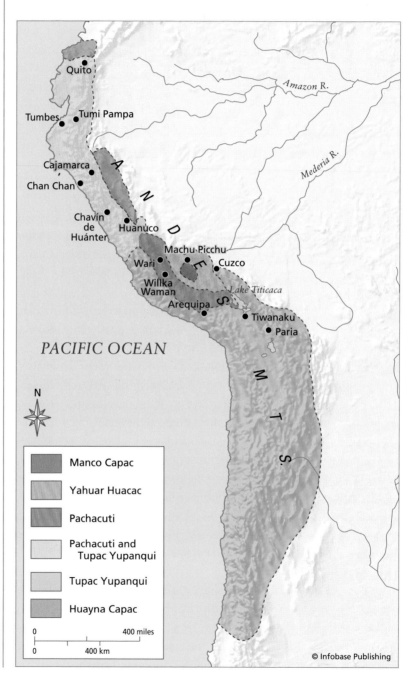

Manco Capac

Yahuar Huacac

Pachacuti

Pachacuti and
Tupac Yupanqui

Tupac Yupanqui

Huayna Capac

© Infobase Publishing

Occasionally, little rebellions needed to be put down. Pachacuti used a concept called *mitima* to eliminate dissent. *Mitima* means "resettlement." An entire village or sections of that village were forcibly moved from their home to new, pro-Inca locations. *Mitima* broke up the rebels yet did not deprive the village of needed services, since loyal Inca workers moved in to replace the rebels and maintain normal levels of productivity.

Mitima was also used for some agricultural groups. There are several cases where villages designated for resettlement were moved to places that the Inca wanted to rework and develop, such as the terraced maize (a type of corn) fields in Cochabamba.

CLIMATE AND AGRICULTURE

The Inca Empire began and expanded high in the Andes Mountains. The mountains form three distinct ranges: the Cordillera Oriental to the east, the Cordillera Occidental to the west, and the Cordillera Central. Broad, sweeping valleys carved by the region's many rivers and streams spread between the different mountain ranges. These mountain streams are the source of the three great river systems of South America: the Amazon, which flows through Peru and Brazil; the Orinoco of Colombia and Venezuela; and the Parana-Paraguay-Uruguay river system.

The region is broken up into four distinct climate zones: the *yunga*, the *quechua*, the *suni*, and the *puna*. Each zone supports different plants and animals, although some species can survive in several zones. Just as in Inca times, today's Andean people cope with extreme climate changes and high altitudes.

The *yunga* zone rises from the foothills of the Andes up to 5,000 feet. The region incorporates the western foothills and is generally warmer and drier than other Andes regions. In this zone, the Incas built raised fields crisscrossed with irrigation ditches that enabled them to bring water to the fields. This increased crop yields.

In its natural state, the *yunga* is a semi-arid (receiving low annual rainfall) grassland with low shrubs, cactus, and grasses. However, civilizations that lived long before the Incas cleared the land for agriculture. Corn, potatoes, beans, fruit, and grain—the main crops of the Inca culture—continue to provide food for today's Peruvian farmers.

Terraced farms and storehouses line the steep hillsides near Machu Picchu. Inca farmland built in this way is still in use in Peru today.

The *quechua* zone begins where the *yunga* ends, rising from about 5,000 to 11,500 feet. Early cultures transformed forest into farmland in the *quechua* zone. The region has moderate temperatures with enough rainfall. Common crops in the *quechua* are the same today as they were in the Inca days: many varieties of corn and potatoes, quinoa (a plant grown for its seeds), amaranth (a type of grain), squash, lima beans, and fruit.

Above the *quechua* zone lies the *suni*, soaring more than 11,500 feet above sea level. High mountain valleys once supported vast grasslands that were cleared for planting high-altitude crops. Common crops in the *suni* include corn, potatoes, oca (a root vegetable), grains, and other hardy crops. As in Inca days, natives in the *suni* today herd llamas and alpacas. Temperatures are far colder in the *suni* than in the lower zones. Soaring above the *suni* is the *puna*, a cold zone where few crops grow.

In the east, the Andes drop into dense Amazon rainforest where the land has changed little since the days of Inca rule. Inca farmers knew how to grow high-altitude crops in regions with limited rainfall. In the dense tropical atmosphere of the Amazon, however, rain fell inches at a time and rivers flooded their banks. The Incas hated the climate.

The Incas used some of this land to grow coca, a medicinal herb used to improve stamina and reduce pain. The jungle was so hot and wet to the Inca people that being sent to the coca fields was considered a terrible punishment. However, the region produced a variety of unusual fruits and vegetables prized by the Incas: manioc (a root vegetable), sweet potatoes, avocados, guavas, and pineapples. These foods still form the main diet for many of the groups of Native peoples who live in the Amazon region.

Toward the southern end of the empire, the mountains fall away into sweeping grasslands, called pampas, much like the tallgrass prairies of North America. The grasses in this region send roots several feet

CONNECTIONS

Applying Inca Agricultural Technology

The Incas used every possible square foot of arable land (land that can be farmed) to produce food, and developed ways to transform unusable land. These included terracing (building farmable plots on the sides of mountains), building raised planting platforms, draining marshy areas, and irrigating (bringing water to) dry fields. Millions of hours of labor were spent clearing land, erecting stone walls, and filling the terraces with soil. Modern agronomists (people who study farming methods) wondered if all that work produced good results.

In 1983, Dr. Clark Erickson of the University of Pennsylvania headed up a team of agronomists who decided to duplicate Inca agricultural methods. They recreated Inca farm terraces and grew crops traditional to Inca farming: potatoes and quinoa (a plant grown for its seeds).

The results amazed the scientists. Normally, when potatoes are planted on a plot that size, the result is about eight tons of potatoes per acre. The 1984 potato crop in the Inca beds produced more than 16 tons per acre. And the following year it produced 30 tons per acre.

It is no wonder that many Inca-built agricultural terraces in the Andes Mountains are still in use today. They are space-saving and effective. Andes farmers continue to get high crop yields from an agricultural plan devised in the 1400s.

into the soil. Inca farmers had only primitive wooden ploughs, operated by forcing the blade into the soil with the foot. With just these foot ploughs, Inca farmers had great difficulty cutting through the thick native grasses to clear land for crops. Thus, the most densely packed grasslands were left intact and thrive today as one of the world's most valued natural grassland ecosystems.

The western quarter lay along South America's western coast. It is an odd place where the world's driest desert (the Atacama) is right next to the world's largest ocean (the Pacific). The region is south of the Equator, so winds blow from east to west. Rain clouds travel from the Brazilian and Argentinean coasts toward the Andes Mountains to the west, dumping rainfall on the dense tropical forests. Farther west,

CONNECTIONS

A Living Language

Quexhua, the language of the Inca Empire, is still spoken by 8 to 10 million people living in the Andes today. This means one-fourth of Peru's population and a large number of people in Ecuador speak Quechua. The language has changed since Inca times, though. When the Spanish arrived in the 1500s, they created a written form for Quechua. Until then, Quechua existed only as a spoken language.

Today's Quechua has three vowels: *a*, *i*, and *u*. Much like English, the vowels can have different sounds. The *i*, for example, may be spoken as a long *i* (as in bike), short *i* (pit), or short *e* (set). Spellings that appear with *e* or *o* in them are often influenced by the Spanish language. This can make things confusing, because the same word might be spelled two ways. For example, both *qumir* and *qomer* mean "green."

There are fewer consonants in Quechua than there are in English. They include *ch*,

f, h, k, l, m, n, p, q, r, s, t, w, and *y*. Spanish influence added *ñ* (pronounced *nya*), and *ll* (pronounced *ya*). The way the consonants are pronounced in Quecha is a lot like the way they are pronounced in English, so English speakers have an easy time learning Quechua.

An interesting aspect of Quechua is that speakers can indicate how sure they are about something simply by changing a noun. For example, a speaker can add the letter *m* as an ending to a noun to show definite knowledge, or add an *s* to show that the speaker heard something about the topic but does not personally know it to be true. Thus, the sentence *Tayta Amaru karpintirum* means "Amaru is a carpenter," indicating that the speaker personally knows Amaru's profession. *Tayta Amaru karpintirus*, on the other hand, means someone else told the speaker that "Amaru is a carpenter."

the mountains block rainfall from the western desert regions, leaving a desert so dry that even cactus cannot survive and corpses dehydrate into natural mummies.

Small rivers such as the Tambo, Ica, and Santa cut fertile valleys through the dry western region. The rivers served as the lifeblood for cultures settling in the area. By 3000 B.C.E., people had cleared forest to expand farmland. Extensive farming began long before the Incas ruled the region.

COMMUNICATIONS

When an empire expands to the size of the Inca Empire, there can be problems with communications. To overcome this problem, Pachacuti ordered that all people under his rule must know how to speak Quechua. They could continue speaking their own language in their everyday lives, as long as they knew the language of the Incas. Children began learning Quechua at birth. Within a short time, all Inca citizens could speak with one another, regardless of background or rank.

Roughly 15,000 miles of roads connected the various districts of the empire. To keep communications open between each region, the Inca culture established a system of runners, called *chasquis*. These runners were stationed at short distances along the roads. The *chasquis* were trained to memorize and deliver messages exactly as they were given. The runners traveled day and night, so a message could be sent from the farthest reaches of the empire—more than 2,000 miles—and arrive in Cuzco in about a week. This is about the same amount of time it takes a letter to travel 3,000 miles by today's modern postal service.

REBUILDING CUZCO

Once Pachacuti turned over military leadership to his son Tupac Yupanqui, he dedicated his time to rebuilding Cuzco. He wanted the city to stand as a symbol of Inca power and skill, and he imagined a city that would become a model of architecture, planning, and construction.

Since the city is about 11,680 feet above sea level, building projects were very difficult for the workers. The higher up in the mountains, the less oxygen is in the air, making it difficult to breathe. The winters

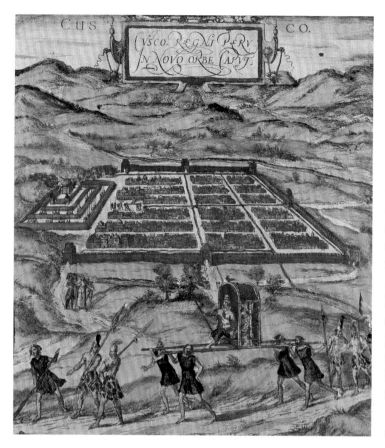

The Spanish drew the first representations of Inca cities and culture, such as this view of Cuzco as it was during Inca times.

are cold, and stone construction requires millions of work hours. By the time the Spanish arrived in 1532, Cuzco's center included about 4,000 solidly built stone structures, with much of that work accomplished in just 60 years.

The city plan took the shape of a puma, an animal much admired by the Inca culture for its strength and cunning. The puma shape of Cuzco can still be seen in photos taken from airplanes. At the puma's head, Pachacuti built the fortress-temple of Sacsahuaman. In the center, royal palaces and huge public plazas took shape. In the tail, there were homes for nobles and the central temple, the Coricancha.

The city had a complex sewer and water system, built with stone-lined trenches. Fresh water was drawn from nearby rivers—the Huatanay and the Tullamayo—that Inca engineers had diverted by building canals. Engineers also built wells to hot springs beneath the earth to provide hot baths for royalty.

The citadel (a high fortress) of Sacsahuaman provided protection in several ways. It stood on a hill from which guards could see long distances. In case of an attack from any direction, guards warned Cuzco's citizens, who then moved into the fortress. The fortress had three major towers, one for the Sapa Inca, and the other two for the military. Sacsahuaman got fresh water from underground streams, and stored enough food and clothing so that a siege of the fortress would be useless. Sacsahuaman was also a temple for prayer and sacrifices.

The Coricancha replaced the Intihuasi built by earlier Sapa Incas. The main temple, dedicated to the sun god, Inti, was literally wallpa-

The Coricancha Revealed

Inca masons gained such skill with shaping and matching stones that, even today, many walls built under Inca rule still stand. They have survived countless earthquakes, a brutal climate, and the destructive conquest of the Spaniards.

In fact, in May 1950, a major earthquake shook the city of Cuzco to its foundations. The 400-year-old Church of Santo Domingo, built by the Spanish, crumbled. The Spanish had built their church over the Coricancha, the main Inca temple. Beneath the rubble of Santo Domingo lay the foundations of the Coricancha—still standing and rock-solid.

Efforts to preserve and rebuild the Spanish church met with resistance, because some people claimed the Coricancha had as much importance in Peruvian culture as the Roman Catholic church. The movement to recapture Inca heritage won in this case, and the Coricancha's walls remain.

pered with sheets of gold—the "sweat of the sun"—and the roof was made of a blend of golden straw, natural reeds, grasses, and stems. There were six buildings in all, with the other buildings set up as temples to the Incas' other main gods: the moon, stars, thunder, lightning, and rainbows. Daily services and sacrifices were made to the gods in the main temple.

Only priests and nobility could enter the Coricancha. The Acllahuasi—the house of the *acllas*—and the school for young men were also located in the city center near the Coricancha.

Guarded gates controlled entrances to Cuzco, and no one could enter the city between sunset and sunrise. The city center where the palaces were located was reserved for the Sapa Inca, his family, servants, and the households of past Sapa Incas. However, when major religious events took place, both nobles and peasants filled the central plazas across from the palace to watch.

The city was a masterpiece of design, innovation, and planning. It had three primary districts: urban, suburban, and rural. A garden-forest separated the urban center from the outlying suburban towns. Neighborhoods or districts divided the urban area where ethnic groups, such as conquered people from the west or north, lived in specific areas set aside for them. Their clothing distinguished them from people of other districts, since no one was allowed to wear the clothes or headgear of any other ethnic group. In this way, guards knew who belonged in which district and kept a close watch on citizens' movements. Laws prevented people from moving from their designated area to another ethnic district.

Suburban towns, evenly spaced about six miles apart, provided homes for farmers, miners, and other workers. Roads connected each town to its neighboring villages and to the city center.

In his book, *Inca and Spaniard,* historian Albert Marrin describes the city: "Cuzco was laid out in a huge checkerboard. Its streets were narrow and paved with stone. In addition, four main roads, one for each of the empire's 'quarters,' began at Joy Square, an open space of 20 acres at the city's center. . . . The House of Learning and the palaces of Sapa Incas, living and dead, surrounded Joy Square on three sides. These buildings, made of stone blocks, many weighing 20 tons, were marvels of engineering."

A LUXURIOUS LIFESTYLE

Although Pachacuti was a talented and wise ruler, he was still as arrogant and privileged as any king. He never walked anywhere. Instead, he traveled in a litter decorated with gold and gems and carried by more than a dozen servants. Other servants traveled in front of the litter making sure the path was smooth, so the Inca ruler would not be jostled during his travels. When he ate, his food was served on gold or silver plates, and since he did almost nothing for himself, his secondary wives or concubines fed him. They even collected his spit in their hands.

Gold poured into Cuzco every year, mined in various places in the Andes. It was used for decorating the Coricancha and for the palaces of the Sapa Inca. In Cuzco, skilled goldsmiths and artisans turned the gold into plates, utensils, bowls, statues, jewelry, and other objects.

Despite the vast amounts of gold, the Incas did not place the highest value on precious metals or gemstones. They valued cloth above even gold and jewels because of the amount of work involved in producing truly fine cloth. Cloth was worth so much that it was never cut. The garments worn by the people were woven with the armholes and the opening for the head as part of the pattern. The finer the fabric, the greater was its value. The government accepted fine weaving as tax payment. It used the cloth given in taxes for paying the military.

Nobles of the Inca court wore luxurious clothing and golden crowns and jewelry. But nothing was as ornate as the clothing of the Sapa Inca himself.

Women spun thread and wove every day, even using their free time, such as when they were walking from their homes to the fields, for spinning yarn. Weaving was done on a backstrap loom attached to the body. A loom has a warp (the vertical threads) and a weft (the horizontal threads). With a backstrap loom, warp threads are held tight between an anchor (a door or tree, for example, or even another person) and the weaver's body. The body anchor is called a backstrap.

IN THEIR OWN WORDS

The Death of Pachacuti

In the book *History of the Incas*, 16th century historian and navigator Pedro Sarmiento De Gamboa describes the death of the greatest Sapa Inca ("unique chief"). Clements Markham of the Hakluyt Society (a society dedicated to the advancement of knowledge and education regarding world history) translated this section of the book in 1907:

> Being in the highest prosperity and sovereignty of his life, he [Pachacuti] fell ill . . . and, feeling that he was at the point of death, he sent for all his sons who were then in the city [of Cuzco]. In their presence he first divided all his jewels and contents of his wardrobe. Next, he made them plough furrows [rows in the field to plant seeds] in token that they were vassals [servants] of their brother, and that they had to eat by the sweat of their hands. He also gave them arms in token that they were to fight for their brother. He then dismissed them.
>
> He next sent for the Incas orejones [noblemen] of Cuzco, his relations, and for Tupac Inca his son to whom he spoke, with a few words, in this manner: "Son! you now see how many great nations I leave to you, and you know what labor they have cost me. Mind that you are the man to keep and augment them. No one must raise his two eyes against you and live, even if he be your own brother. I leave you these our relations that they may be your councilors. Care for them and they shall serve you. . . . Have my golden image in the House of the Sun, and make my subjects, in all the provinces, offer up solemn sacrifice, after which keep the feast of purucaya [a burial ceremony], that I may go to rest with my father the Sun." Having finished his speech, they say that he began to sing in a low and sad voice with words of his own language. They are as follows:
>
> I was born as a flower of the field,
> As a flower I was cherished in my youth,
> I came to my full age, I grew old,
> Now I am withered and die.
> Having uttered these words, he laid his head upon a pillow and expired. . . .

(Source: Sarmiento De Gamboa, Pedro. *History of the Incas*. Mineola, N.Y.: Dover Publications, 1999.)

The weaver uses a shuttle to run the weft threads over and under the warp threads, working from the body forward. Thus, the length of the weaver's arms limited the length of fabric that was produced—the cloth was never longer than the arms of the woman who wove it.

Some men and religious women became expert weavers. They were employed by the government to produce cloth that could be used as gifts or when negotiating an enemy's surrender. Cloth became an important part of the religious rituals made to the Inca gods. Daily, yards of fine quality cloth were burned on the altars of Inti, the sun god.

The Inca ruler wore a complicated woven tunic (a loose garment that usually reached to the wearer's knees) of *cumbi*, a vicuña wool fabric made from a wild relative of the llama and worn only by nobles. On his head he wore a *llautu*, a braided crown with tassels and feathers. Thus dressed and seated on a stool made of gold, the Sapa Inca received people who wanted to speak with him.

No person dared look into the face of the Sapa Inca, because he was considered divine and the "son of the sun," and to look directly at him was unacceptable. Even the highest noble approached the Inca in a crouch with a bundle on his back. This bundle could be small or large and represented the fact that the approaching person did not consider himself equal to the Sapa Inca.

TUPAC YUPANQUI

When Pachacuti died in 1471, his son Tupac Yupanqui became the next Sapa Inca. Tupac Yupanqui had already established himself as a skilled military leader. In 1460, while his father was still Sapa Inca, he conquered the Chimú people. This culture lived in the Moche Valley from 1300 to 1460. As they had done with many earlier cultures, the Incas absorbed the best of what the Chimú had to offer.

The Chimú were artisans who worked with gold and silver, turquoise and lapis lazuli (a blue precious stone). In a Chimú city, nearly one-third of the citizens may have been craftspeople producing complex beaded collars, gold masks and crowns set with gems, religious images, jeweled plates and utensils, and personal jewelry for nobles. Goldsmiths and silversmiths knew how to create alloys (blends of various metals) and how to use heat to fuse metal parts together. Artists created brilliant mosaics (pictures made with pieces of colored tile) to decorate city buildings.

The Chimú city of Chan Chan was the largest city in pre-modern South America. Architects designed the city around 10 quadrangles (four-sided open spaces) with each quadrangle featuring homes, workshops, storehouses, gardens, and reservoirs.

Chimú forts manned with experienced warriors defended the kingdom's roads. The culture supported a powerful military state with only one flaw: The Chimú depended on aqueducts to carry water to irrigate their land. When Tupac Yupanqui led Inca warriors against the Chimú in 1460, the Incas attacked by cutting off the water supply. The Chimú surrendered and the Incas took over. Tupac Yupanqui added Chimú artists and craftspeople to the Inca labor force.

As Sapa Inca, Tupac Yupanqui had many of the same leadership skills and vision as his father. His name—which means "The Unforgettable One"—represents his ability on the battlefield and as a government leader.

Tupac Yupanqui was a merciless, brutal warrior. Albert Marrin writes in his book, *Inca and Spaniard: Pizarro and the Conquest of Peru*, "When the coastal city of Huarco resisted too long, he decided to make an example of those who defied him. He promised the Huarcans fair treatment in return for their surrender. But as they left the safety of their walls, he attacked. Thousands were killed on the spot or hung from the walls; piles of their bleached bones littered the ground for generations."

After a short reign of only 22 years, Tupac Yupanqui died in 1493. After his death, a number of possible leaders emerged, along with a period of fighting that ended when Huayna Capac, one of Tupac Yupanqui's sons, took charge and declared himself Sapa Inca.

In 1653, historian and Inca Cronista Father Bernabé Cobo, in his *History of the New World*, described Huayna Capac as an able and popular leader: "He was much loved by his vassals and held to be valiant and firm. He achieved many and renowned victories; he broadened the borders of his empire with many provinces that he added to it. He showed himself to be as prudent in government as he was vigorous at arms. . . ."

The Inca Empire reached its largest size under the leadership of Huayna Capac. He led his army in conquering the Chachapoyas and Cayambes tribes of present-day Ecuador, even though both tribes had reputations for brutality and savage war tactics. Unlike his grandfather,

Pachacuti, Huayna Capac thought he could divide the empire and rule from two capitals. He planned to make Quito (in modern Ecuador) into a northern capital that was equal in all ways to Cuzco. It turned out to be a mistake. This plan eventually led to the end of Inca rule in the Andes.

CHAPTER 3

THE FINAL YEARS OF INCA RULE

WHILE HE WAS IN THE NORTHERN CAPITAL OF QUITO, INCA ruler Huayna Capac heard about strange people who had come to his land. They were white men with dark hair and beards. Since beards were rare among natives of the Andes Mountains, facial hair must have seemed bizarre to the Incas. The men were described accurately as wearing hats and vests of metal (European style armor), riding upon large beasts (horses), and carrying weapons unknown to the Incas.

The news frightened Huayna Capac, who believed in omens (signs or events that tell the future) and fortunes. He recalled a time when he had seen omens in the sky, which he believed predicted a great disaster that would fall upon the Incas. The priest who had read the omens warned that the empire, its religion, and its laws would die.

Huayna Capac believed that the arrival of these strangers to his land fulfilled this omen. He never actually met any Spaniards in person. But in 1525 he died from one of the things the Spanish brought with them—the deadly disease smallpox.

From 1518 to 1527, smallpox swept across the Caribbean and Central America and headed south toward the Inca Empire. Up to this point, the Inca Empire had been somewhat isolated. They had been assimilating (taking in and absorbing) neighboring cultures but never ventured far beyond the Inca borders.

When smallpox came, the Inca people were astounded. They had no experience with this disease, and so no immunity, no medicine to fight it, and no knowledge of what had caused it. The disease first

OPPOSITE
Francisco Pizarro (shown here in an anonymous 16th-century European etching) conquered the Inca Empire by taking advantage of the chaos caused by two brothers' battle for the title of Sapa Inca.

arrived in Cuzco, brought, perhaps, by travelers through the region. Within a short time, smallpox spread throughout the empire, leaving thousands dead.

Huayna Capac became so sick that he was not thinking clearly, and he named his infant son, Ninan, as his heir to the throne. Considering Ninan's age, it would have been impossible for him to rule. But in any case, the heir contracted smallpox, too, and died in 1525 just a few days after his father. This left two of Huayna Capac's other sons, Atahuallpa and Huáscar, fighting over who would be the next Sapa Inca.

CIVIL WAR

The Inca Empire, once a mighty power, was now struggling through a civil war in which both Huáscar and Atahuallpa claimed the throne and were ready to fight for it.

Huáscar made the first move by sending his army to confront Atahuallpa's troops. Four captains led Huáscar's imperial army: Hango, Atoc, Aguapante, and Cuxi Yupanque. After the first major battle, Hango and Atoc lay dead on the battlefield, Cuxi Yupanque had been captured, and Aguapante escaped. He was captured and imprisoned, then escaped again.

The loss to his younger brother enraged Huáscar. He declared Atahuallpa to be *auca*—a treasonous enemy—and immediately sent a larger army of 15,000 to attack. The battles swung back and forth. Huáscar sent larger and larger armies, each of which was defeated by Atahuallpa and his men. Finally, Huáscar himself went to war with a massive army, only to suffer the same defeat. Atahuallpa's army was far too experienced for Huáscar.

As the new self-appointed king, Atahuallpa revealed his true nature. He pretended that he wished to return Huáscar to the throne and called the Capac Incas (nobles who were directly descended from Manco Capac, the first Sapa Inca) to Cuzco for the event. These nobles were the military leaders, governors, and administrators of the empire. Most were loyal to Huáscar, because they were his direct relatives. They belonged to a closely-knit group called a *panaca*.

All arrived in Cuzco on the set date, "except for those—and they were few—who continued to mistrust this prince," says Cronista Gar-

IN THEIR OWN WORDS

A Dark Prophecy

One night during Inca ruler Huayna Capac's reign, three rings—red, green, and brown—were seen encircling the moon in the sky over Cuzco. The priest who interpreted the omens believed that they predicted disaster for the Sapa Inca, his family, and his people. He was right. His prophecy was preserved in oral tradition, and eventually written down by the *cronistas*:

> *Oh, my only lord, know you that your mother the Moon, who is always merciful, warns you that the great Pachacamac, creator and support of the entire universe, threatens your family and your Empire with great trials that he will soon visit upon you. For this first blood-colored ring, surrounding your mother, means that a very cruel war will break out among your descendants, after you will have departed to rest beside your father the Sun; your royal blood will be shed in such streams that after a few years, nothing will remain of it. The black ring threatens your religion, your laws and the Empire, which will not survive these wars, and the death of your people; and all you have done, and all your ancestors have done, will vanish in smoke, as is shown by the third ring.*

(Source: Marrin, Albert. *Inca and Spaniard: Pizarro and the Conquest of Peru*. New York: Macmillan Publishing Company, 1989.)

cilaso de la Vega. "And when they were all gathered together, Atahuallpa gave orders that every last one of them should be put to death; for, in reality, it was in this way that he intended to make sure that the future would be his." Thus, Atahuallpa eliminated any possible rivals for the title of Sapa Inca.

Atahuallpa also had the mummy of the *panaca's* ancestor, Tupac Yupanqui, burned. Inca subjects worshipped the mummies of former Sapa Incas as gods. After all, a Sapa Inca was a "son of the sun," or a living god. Thus, by destroying the mummy and the principal leaders of the *panaca*, Atahuallpa destroyed any hope the *panaca* may have had of rising up against him in the future.

When the Spanish arrived in 1527, they did not have to spend much time conquering the Inca Empire. The civil war had divided the empire and created chaos. No one was certain who the Sapa Inca was. The political, administrative, and military systems of the Inca Empire, which relied on clear instructions from the Sapa Inca, were unable to respond effectively when the Spanish attacked.

THE CONQUISTADORS

As the Spanish conquistadors (conquerors) spread across North and South America—the region they called the New World—they caused destruction and death. They came to get gold, and they did not mind stealing it from Native American cultures. In 1521, the Spanish destroyed the Aztec capital of Tenochtitlán, in present-day Mexico. Piles of Aztec gold made the conquistador Hernán Cortés a rich man. Other conquistadors grew bitter with jealousy and greed.

Among the Spaniards seeking fame and fortune were Francisco Pizarro (ca. 1475–1541), the illegitimate son of an army captain, and Diego de Almagro (1475–1538), who became Pizarro's financial partner. In 1524, the pair made their first exploration southward in search of gold and gems. The trip was a terrible failure. The expedition of about 80 men slogged through dense mangrove swamps, suffered from countless insect attacks, and quickly dismissed any thought that the land south of Panama (the most southern country of Central America) offered wealth that was worth having.

Despite their failure, the partners funded a second voyage, drawn by the promise of finding gold. With two ships and 160 men, Pizarro and Almagro sailed in November 1526, heading toward the San Juan River in present-day Colombia. At some point, Almagro decided to return to Panama for additional supplies and men, while Pizarro and his men camped at the river's edge.

The first encounter with Native people occurred while Almagro was gone. Pizarro's pilot, named Ruiz, spotted a large raft sailing on the river with a crew of 20 sailors and a

IN THEIR OWN WORDS

The Final Battle

Cronista Garcilaso de la Vega described the final battle in about 1532 between Atahuallpa's army and Huáscar's this way:

Atahuallpa's generals had a clear understanding of the situation; their fortunes depended on their speed. So they immediately sought out Huáscar, in order to engage him in battle before he should have received more numerous reinforcements . . . . No peace offers preceded the fighting, and it immediately became a terrible melee that lasted all day . . . . The king was obliged to flee with what was left of his guard, reduced now to 1,000 men, at the most. Atahuallpa's army soon overtook and captured him; and thus it was that Huáscar, having been made a prisoner by his brother's generals, saw the last of his faithful troops meet death before his very eyes.

(Source: de la Vega, Garcilaso. *The Incas: The Royal Commentaries of the Inca Garcilaso de la Vega*. Translated by Maria Jolas from the critical, annotated edition of Alain Gheerbrant. New York: The Orion Press, 1961.)

number of passengers. The encounter sparked the Spaniards' interest because the people were dressed in fine clothes and wore elegant gold and silver jewelry. They saw drinking vessels encrusted with gems, silver mirrors, and finely woven and embroidered cotton and wool cloth. By using hand signals, the traders explained that the gold and gems came from a land far to the south. The Spanish were dazzled.

In mid-1527, Pizarro and his men found themselves camped once more in a location buzzing with biting insects—the Isla del Gallo, or Isle of the Rooster. The situation grew increasingly desperate, because food was scarce, the sun burned the soldiers' skin, and many became sick with disease. Poisonous snakes infested the swampy camp and the starving men ate them, contributing to their ill health.

Pizarro kept his men together by encouraging them to fish and hunt, and gather fruit and berries. Pizzaro was an able, experienced soldier. But he could also be very cruel. Pizarro had tortured and burned local chiefs in an effort to get those men to reveal where they kept the tribe's gold, silver, and gems. But they would reveal nothing.

By August 1527, a handful of Pizzaro's men were dying every week. The few who survived were eager to give up any promise of future wealth and return to Panama. Many prepared to overthrow their captain, but Pizarro would not give up his search for riches. Historian Carmen Bernand writes in his book, *The Incas: People of the Sun*, that Pizarro drew a line in the sand with his sword, saying, "Comrades and friends, on this side lie poverty, hunger, effort, torrential rains, and privation. On that side lies pleasure. On this side, we return to Panama and poverty. On that side, we become rich."

Thirteen chose to follow Pizarro's path to promised wealth. The rest returned to Panama, taking the sailing ship with them. For seven

ATAHUALLPA, INCA XIIII.

This 16th-century European portrait of Atahuallpa, the last Sapa Inca, shows him with a traditional Inca battleaxe.

The First Encounter

The first discussion between the *curaca* (government employee) of the village of Tumbes and the Spanish visitors was recorded by Francisco Pizarro's secretary, Francisco de Xeres, in *The Conquest of Peru*.

> *He [the curaca] asked the captain where were they from, what land they had come from, and what were they looking for, or what was their purpose in going by seas and land without stopping? Francisco Pizarro replied that they had come from Spain, where they were native, and that in that land there was a great and powerful king called Charles, whose vassal and servants they were, and many others because he ruled wide territories. They had left their land to explore these parts, as they could see, and to place what they found under their king's authority, but primarily, and above all, to let them know that the idols they worshiped were false, and that to save their souls, they have to become Christians and believe in the God the Spanish worshiped.*

(Source: de Xeres, Francisco. *The Conquest of Peru* (1534). Translated by Clements R. Markham. London: Hakluyt Society, 1970.)

months, Pizzaro's men had little to eat, endured the terrible heat, and suffered from the diseases malaria and dysentery. They did not know that farther to the south, the Inca Empire had greater wealth in gold, silver, and gems than any of them had seen before.

Pizarro's partner, Almagro, finally sent a ship to pick up Pizarro and the remaining members of his group. Pizarro was desperate to see the land of riches that had been described to him by local people and the traders on the raft, so he decided they were not ready yet to sail to Panama. Instead, they would sail south.

When the Spanish ship arrived at the coastal village of Tumbes, near today's Ecuadoran border, the townspeople were amazed. They had never before seen a ship or people like this. The Spanish came with horses, and the Inca had never seen those animals, either. The Spaniards were treated as honored guests. The local *curaca* (a government employee) sent a message to Huáscar, one of the two brothers fighting to become Sapa Inca, telling him that strangers had arrived in the Inca land.

CAPTURE AT CAJAMARCA

When Pizarro first arrived in Tumbes in 1528, the empire was in the middle of a civil war. Pizarro, who had come with only a small force, decided to head north again, leaving the brothers, Huáscar and Atahuallpa, to their dispute. In 1531, Pizarro returned to Tumbes. This time he had more soldiers, more horses, and more weapons. This larger force numbered fewer than 160 men, but Pizarro believed this was all he needed.

While Pizarro wisely waited, Huáscar and Atahuallpa destroyed each other's armies. In 1532, Pizarro approached the city of Cajamarca in the northern part of the Inca Empire. Atahuallpa had taken the throne and was camped on a nearby hill. This was Pizarro's opportunity to meet the Sapa Inca. He waited all day in the city for Atahuallpa to arrive. As the sun set, Atahuallpa left his hilltop camp. Some historians claim that Atahuallpa believed that the magic of the strangers—their arquebuses (guns)—would not work at night, so he waited until then for the meeting.

Atahuallpa arrived carried on a gold and silver litter set with jewels. A dozen or so servants went before him, sweeping the road to make sure that no pebble should make their lord's journey bumpy. Troops stood in the main plaza around the Sapa Inca, singing songs that honored their leader.

The Spaniards waited until one of Atahuallpa's captains signaled for them to approach the Sapa Inca. Pizarro did so, along with a Spanish priest named Fra Vincente de Valverde. The priest carried a Bible in one hand and a crucifix in the other. According to Francisco de Xeres, Pizarro's secretary, in his book *The Conquest of Peru*, the priest said, "I am a priest of God, and I teach Christians the things of God, and in like manner I come to teach you. What I teach is that which God says to us in this book."

Atahuallpa looked at the book, but the contents meant nothing to him. The Inca had no written language, so the idea of a book was foreign to him. Atahuallpa threw the Bible away, telling the priest that he knew about the Spaniards and how they had taken food and cloth from Inca warehouses and treated Inca chiefs with contempt. Atahuallpa ordered the Spanish to return all that they had taken, and refused to leave the plaza until it was done.

Pizarro made a split-second decision to attack Atahuallpa. He put on his armor and raised his sword and dagger (a fighting knife). Although Atahuallpa had more than a thousand soldiers standing by, Pizarro and four brave soldiers advanced to Atahuallpa's litter on horseback. Horses (animals that are not native to the Americas) were strange and wondrous beasts to the Incas, and the Inca guard fell back as the Spaniards charged. The guard surrounding Atahuallpa was killed and the Sapa Inca was taken captive. Atahuallpa's army, with no one at the top to give orders, did not make a move. Pizarro and his men were able to take the city unopposed.

Pizarro then told Atahuallpa not to be humiliated by losing to a troop of only five men. He boasted that he, Pizarro, had conquered greater kingdoms than the Inca Empire with just five men—which was not true. He explained that the Christian God that he followed supported Pizarro in his desire to convert the Incas to Christianity. Accord-

The missionary Felipe Guaman Poma de Ayala made this drawing showing the first meeting in 1532 of Pizarro (kneeling left in a helmet) and Atahuallpa (center with a headdress).

ing to Xeres, Pizarro said, "Our Lord permitted that your pride should be brought low, and that no Indian should be able to offend a Christian."

Pizarro then demanded a ransom of enough gold to fill a storeroom in the building where Atahuallpa was being held. Atahuallpa, insulted that the ransom should be so small, claimed that he would give even more gold to his captives if it would purchase his freedom. After all, what was gold to the Incas? They valued cloth far more than any metal because of the amount of work involved in producing it.

While Pizarro held Atahuallpa captive, Atahuallpa's men continued to hold Huáscar. Atahuallpa learned through his jailers that Huáscar promised the Spaniards even more gold, silver, and gemstones than Atahuallpa had offered to restore him to the throne. The young Sapa Inca sent word to his men to execute Huáscar.

According to historians, the imprisoned Huáscar realized his brother's captains had orders to execute him. Just before he died in 1532, Huáscar said, "I was lord and master of this land for only a very short time, but my traitorous brother, upon whose orders I shall soon die, despite the fact that I am his legitimate lord, will wield the power he usurped for an even shorter time than I did," (as quoted in *The Incas: The Royal Commentaries of the Inca, Garcilaso de la Vega*). Huáscar's last words proved to be true. Atahuallpa, indeed, enjoyed only a very short reign.

With Huáscar out of the way, Atahuallpa expected to pay his ransom, regain his throne, and kill all the Spaniards. Cronista Juan de Betanzos said in *Narrative of the Incas*, "Atahuallpa gathered or caused the amassing of all the gold and silver that he had promised, and as he gathered it Atahuallpa pleaded with the marquis [nobleman] not to allow any of his men to damage or destroy any piece of gold or silver that he placed there or caused to be gathered. Atahuallpa's intention must have been to unleash such a war when he was freed that he would once again see his gold and silver items." However, once the treasure was safely in Pizarro's hands, the Spaniard did not release his captive.

Pizarro finally had enough gold and silver to make him a rich man. However, after Pizarro and his men had suffered near starvation, insects, disease, and discomfort, his former partner, Almagro, arrived just in time to collect his portion of the wealth. In 1533, the treasure was divided up, and King Charles I's (r. 1516–1556) share was sent back to Spain with Hernando Pizarro, half-brother of Francisco Pizarro.

A Loss Far Greater Than Gold

Inca ruler Atahuallpa's ransom weighed in at 13,420 pounds of gold and 26,000 pounds of silver, all of it in finely crafted items. Unfortunately, Pizarro saw only the precious metal and not the valuable emblems of Inca heritage. He ordered his men to melt down every piece into bars, called ingots, which could be transported more easily than ornaments. The value of Atahuallpa's ransom, based on average prices of gold ($340 an ounce) and silver ($4.50 an ounce), would be about $75 million today. Recently, an art gallery sold a pair of gold Inca earrings, three inches in diameter, for $17.5 million. Intact as artifacts, Atahuallpa's ransom today would be worth billions.

Atahuallpa was all that remained between Francisco Pizarro and complete conquest of the Inca Empire. Atahuallpa himself had aided the Spaniards by slaughtering anyone else who might have become king and by having his brother executed. With so much to gain, the Spaniards could not resist taking everything.

Almagro and Francisco Pizarro accused Atahuallpa of stealing the throne from his brother, causing the death of the legitimate Inca ruler, making unfair wars against others, causing the deaths of many Inca subjects, having several wives, and taking for himself riches that belonged to the Inca Empire. They staged a trial at which he was judged according to Spanish, not Inca law. Atahuallpa was found guilty of all charges and condemned to death by burning at the stake.

In his book, *The Incas: People of the Sun,* historian Carmen Bernand describes the shock of the sentence and Atahuallpa's reaction: "One cannot imagine a more cruel sentence: The Incas had an absolute terror of cremation because it caused the body to disappear. So Atahuallpa agreed to convert to Catholicism on the condition that he have his head cut off instead."

Atahuallpa converted to Roman Catholicism and was renamed Juan de Atahuallpa. Then Atahuallpa, the last Sapa Inca, was strangled to death. A group of Spaniards who never numbered more than 200 men took over an empire with thousands of subjects.

SPANIARD AGAINST SPANIARD

By 1535, the Spanish had placed Manco Inca (1516–1544), another son of Sapa Inca Huayna Capac, on the Inca throne. But he held no real power and did what the Spanish told him. Meanwhile, Pizarro formed a relationship with the Inca princess Ines Yupanqui, sister of Atahuallpa. Pizarro never officially married Ines, but they did have a daughter whom they named Beatriz. (After Pizarro died, Ines married the Cronista Juan de Betanzos.) Manco Inca remained in Cuzco, where the Inca subjects believed, incorrectly, that he held power.

King Charles V in Spain was thrilled by the amount of gold he received. He rewarded Pizarro and Almagro by dividing the Inca Empire between them. Pizarro received the northern half and Almagro got the south, including Cuzco. Pizarro's share of the Inca wealth made him a very rich man. His power made it possible for him to confiscate Inca land and riches without fear of punishment.

Pizarro headed west, where he built a new city at the mouth of the Rimac River. He named this city Ciudad de los Reyes (Spanish for "City of the Kings"), but it soon came to be called Lima. The layout of the city was quite simple: a series of relatively straight streets that formed more than 100 rectangular city blocks.

In Cuzco, Almagro planned an expedition to investigate his lands in Chile. He left in 1535 and was gone for two years. Manco Inca sent 12,000 Incas to accompany Almagro on his trip. During that time, Pizarro's two half-brothers, Gonzalo and Hernando, decided that the three Pizarro brothers should have the remaining riches in Cuzco. Gonzalo and Hernando Pizarro disliked Almagro. And with Alamagro and 12,000 Incas gone, it was easy for the Pizarro brothers to take whatever they wanted.

Cuzco was filled with Spanish soldiers, which enabled the Pizarro brothers to steal with no fear of any consequences from the Incas. The Spanish looted the Sapa Inca's palace—an act that Francisco Pizarro allowed to go unpunished. Gonzalo then desired Manco Inca's wife, Curo Ocllo. He demanded that Manco Inca hand her over. Instead, Manco Inca presented one of his sisters to Gonzalo, claiming that she was Curo Ocllo.

The Incas, led by Manco Inca, staged an uprising, but it was doomed to failure. They had more soldiers than the Spanish, but inferior weapons. Manco Inca escaped and headed for the rainforests to the east of Cuzco, where he ended up in the remote village of Vilcabamba. Gonzalo Pizarro pursued him for more than two months without success, then returned to Cuzco, ransacked the town, and had the real Curo Ocllo killed. Her body was placed in a floating basket and sent down the Urumbamba River. Gonzalo was certain that Manco Inca's men would find the body. Then the Sapa Inca's desire for revenge would draw him out from his hiding place. But this plan did not work.

In 1539, Almagro returned from his expedition to Chile to find his territory in ruins. Cuzco had been robbed by the Pizarros, many Incas had died, and a siege of Cuzco left thousands either dead or weak from starvation. Almagro and his supporters met the Pizarros in battle. Hernando Pizarro, who had long hated Almagro, ordered his enemy killed. Almagro's death left Cuzco and his other holdings without an owner. The Pizarros grabbed them.

Continued Inca attacks frustrated Spanish efforts to bring the Inca citizens back under control. In his article, "Tupac Amaru, The

Life, Times and Execution of the Last Inca," historian James Q. Jacobs writes, "Seven of Almagro's followers . . . were given refuge by Manco Capac . . . . In 1544 these seven assassinated Manco Inca, their host and protector of two years, by stabbing him in the back while playing horseshoes."

Meanwhile, Hernando Pizarro had to answer for what he and his family had done in Peru. Although King Charles V overlooked much of what the Pizarros had done to the Incas, he could not excuse the execution of Almagro. Hernando Pizarro returned to Spain disgraced, where he spent 22 years in prison. In June 1541, several of Almagro's loyal men broke into Pizarro's official residence and executed him.

SPANISH DOMINION

By the 1540s, the Spanish were firmly in charge in Peru. Efforts to get rid of the conquistadors were not successful. By 1572, the last outpost of the Inca Empire, Vilcabamba, fell into ruin. The Spanish king, Philip II, gave his favorite nobles land and titles in Peru. Under the system of *encomienda*, a Spanish landowner collected taxes from the people

The Roman Catholic Church of Santo Domingo stands on the site of the Coricancha in Cuzco. It retains many Inca features, including the lower walls.

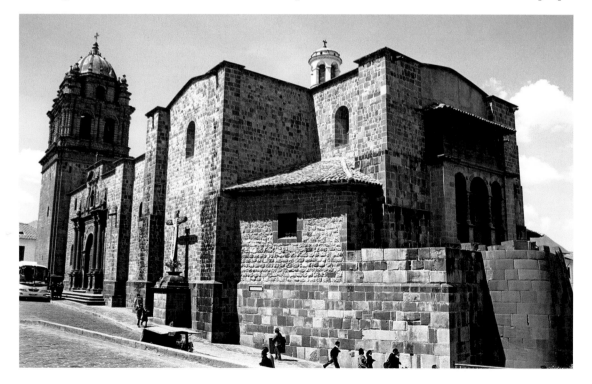

CONNECTIONS

Ancient Customs in Modern Times

Today, Roman Catholicism and Inca tradition blend to create an interesting marriage custom in the Andes Mountains. A contemporary Quechua couple has a Catholic marriage ceremony and is registered in the church records. Before that ceremony takes place, however, courtship and engagement are strictly in the Inca tradition.

The couple becomes engaged after speaking to both sets of parents. At that point, they enter a period of service to each other, called *sirvinakuy*. During this time, the prospective bride works for the groom's family and the groom works for the bride's family, to demonstrate to their future in-laws their willingness to meet the demands of married life. This closely follows the Inca pattern of life in which a new couple became members of the groom's *ayllu* (clan group) and worked within the community. Today, the engaged couple lives together in the home of whichever set of parents has the means and space to house them.

A marriage will not take place until the union has produced a child and shown that the marriage will be fruitful—and even then, weddings can be postponed for several years.

A wedding ceremony costs a great deal and parents and godparents save for years to provide an extravagant event. By the time the new couple reaches the church altar, they may already have two or three children—a fact ignored by the local Catholic priest. Once the couple is married, their children can be baptized and officially become Catholics.

who worked the land. In return, landowners promised protection from attack. But since the only people who might attack were the Spanish, paying them for protection was a joke.

The Roman Catholic Church sent missionaries to convert the "heathens" to Christianity. Priests and friars destroyed Inca idols recklessly, in an attempt to eliminate all signs of idol worship. The people soon learned to hide their knowledge of *huacas* (Inca holy sites, usually found in nature), temples, and religious rituals so the priests would not destroy them.

The priests banned Inca infant, puberty, and marriage rituals, replacing Inca traditions with European customs. Multiple wives for nobles was forbidden, along with the use of feathers, ritual fabrics, burnt offerings to the gods, and even the playing of conch shells at ceremonies. All visible traces of Inca polytheism (worshipping more than one god) were erased, as priests distributed crucifixes and rosary beads by the thousands.

To this day, reverence for all things in nature remains an important part of the Andes culture. The people, although most are Catholic, continue to make small sacrifices to their ancient gods to make sure they have good harvests.

THE LAST TRUE INCA

Despite efforts by the Spanish to wipe out the family line of Sapa Incas, sons of Manco Inca (Sayri Tupac, Tupac Amaru, and Titu Cusi) survived. Sayri Tupac (1535–1561) established an Inca state in the city of Vilcabamba, a refuge in the rainforest.

In 1552, Sayri Tupac received a full pardon for any "crimes" committed against the Spanish. The young emperor of a dead empire accepted the opportunity to leave Vilcabamba and return to Cuzco. Sayri Tupac remained in Cuzco for nine years, where he converted to Christianity and remarried his wife in the Catholic Church. In 1561, Sayri Tupac was poisoned, and the new Inca leader declared Vilcabamba to once again be a rebel state.

Titu Cusi (1530–1570) seized the throne from Sayri Tupac's heir, Tupac Amaru (1544–1572). Titu Cusi became a rebel, attacking Christian travelers and raiding Spanish settlements. The self-proclaimed emperor had good reason to despise the Spanish: They had killed his father and brothers, and raped his aunts, sister, and cousin. He himself had been imprisoned and treated harshly by his Spanish captors.

As he got older, though, Titu Cusi became less interested in resistance and negotiated peace. He promised loyalty to the Spanish king and became a Catholic. He died in 1570, and Tupac Amaru, the last true Inca, took the throne. Again, the Incas rose up against the Spanish.

On June 1, 1572, the first battle for control of the Vilcabamba Valley took place. Within three weeks, the Spanish had advanced into the heart of Vilcabamba, a city that lay in ruins. The people were gone, the buildings burned, and food storage bins destroyed. Tupac Amaru and his followers had disappeared into the jungle.

Three months later, Tupac Amaru was captured and marched into Cuzco. The Spanish tried to convert him to Christianity while, at the same time, he was tried, convicted, and sentenced to hang. The Spanish tortured several of Tupac Amaru's followers to death, then hanged their corpses as a display of their power and ruthlessness.

The Inca's execution became a spectacle, with thousands of Incas around the gallows, wailing over the coming death of their leader. The Spanish viceroy, seeing the crush of the crowd, declared that Tupac Amaru should be immediately beheaded. In his article, "Tupac Amaru, The Life, Times and Execution of the Last Inca," James Q. Jacobs writes, "The Inca's last words were, '*Collanan Pachacamac ricuy auccacuna yahuarniy hichcascancuta.*' Mother Earth, witness how my enemies shed my blood.

"By one account, Tupac Amaru placed his head on the block. The executioner took Tupac's hair in one hand and severed his head in a single blow. He raised his [Tupac's] head in the air for the crowd to view. At the same time all the bells of the many churches and monasteries of the city were rung. A great sorrow and tears were brought to all the native peoples present."

From 1742 to 1761, Juan Santos Atahuallpa attempted a rebellion against Spanish rule. His neo-Inca movement arose because the Spanish treated Peruvians like slaves. The Peruvians farmed land that they did not own and had to pay large fees to do it. There was no way to escape the grinding cycle of poverty that enslaved the Peruvians and made the Spanish wealthy.

Following Juan Santos Atahuallpa, the Peruvian rebels threw a Spanish *corregidor* (royal administrator) and his brother-in-law off a cliff—the time-honored Inca method of punishment. The English, seeking a way to reduce Spanish influence worldwide, provided financial support for the Neo-Inca movement. However, the Spanish were too deeply established in Peru and could not be thrown out. The Neo-Inca effort failed, and the Spanish maintained firm control.

In 1780, José Gabriel Condorcanqui (ca. 1738–1781), who claimed to be a direct descendant of the last true Inca, Tupac Amaru, emerged as the leader of a rebel army numbering nearly 80,000. Their goals were to achieve social reforms in mining and forced labor, and to remove corrupt *corregidores*. Condorcanqui took the name Tupac Amaru II in 1771, and led his followers in repeated attacks against Spanish leaders and mine and plantation owners. Within a year, the Spanish military arrested Tupac Amaru II, held a fake trial, and tortured the rebel leader.

The Spanish revenge against Tupac Amaru II was remarkable for its brutality. The Inca leader watched his wife, son, and comrades executed. On May 18, 1781, Tupac Amaru II spoke his final words to the Spanish viceroy: "There are no accomplices here but you and I. You, the oppressor and I, the liberator. Both of us deserve death!" (as quoted on the Web site "Tupac Amaru II").

The Spanish cut out his tongue then tied him to four horses to tear his body apart. This proved unsuccessful, so the Spanish cut off his head and dismembered the body. They displayed the Inca's severed arms and legs in the main strongholds of Inca rebellion. But they still wanted more revenge. The Spanish hunted down and murdered every relative of Tupac Amaru II, all the way to his fourth cousins. There would be no more rebellions against the Spanish, no more uprisings to restore Inca rule.

PART · II

SOCIETY AND CULTURE

INCA SOCIETY

LIVING AMONG THE INCAS

INCA ART, SCIENCE, AND CULTURE

CHAPTER 4

INCA SOCIETY

THE BIGGER THE INCA EMPIRE GREW, THE MORE DIFFICULT it became to organize, control, and manage its subjects. As new cultures were conquered, the Incas tried to impose their social values and requirements on new Inca subjects. Little rebellions became a common feature of the huge empire, and between the late 1400s and early 1500s, the Inca army was constantly on the move.

Conquered people living on the empire's outer fringes tried to get rid of their new rulers, but they did not succeed. The rigid systems that had brought the Inca Empire to greatness became an unwelcome way of life for some people.

THE GOVERNMENT

The government structure followed a simple plan based on decimal units. Ten households comprised an *ayllu* or clan group. Bachelors, unmarried women, widows, and widowers usually lived with a core family unit. When a man got married, he became a taxpayer, a *puric*, while his wife was listed as a subject and a member of the *ayllu*.

One leader, a *conka camayoc*, made sure everyone within the *ayllu* worked and paid taxes. He also made sure accurate records were kept of births, deaths, marriages, ages of the *ayllu* members, crop yields, and wool and meat from herds of llamas.

To make sure each *conka camayoc* leader did his job, government inspectors toured the regions. The inspectors were called *tokoyricoq*, which means "see-all." They spied on everything from how clean a house was kept to the amount of work produced by an *ayllu*. At every level, there were official government spies to make sure no one cheated the Sapa Inca. This profession was considered honorable, since the spies prevented corruption at every level of the government.

Moving up on the governmental ladder, higher officials oversaw increasingly larger units of households; 20,000 households comprised a province. "Each province had a governor who was responsible for its affairs. There were more than 80 provinces in the Inca Empire, so this added 80 or more administrators to the bureaucracy. Each governor was under the orders of the *apu* of the quarter in which his province lay," says anthropologist Michael Malpass in *Daily Life in the Inca Empire*.

The entire empire was divided into quarters (*suyus*), and each quarter had several provinces. *Apus*, top-ranking officials who were noble relatives of the Sapa Inca, administered the government of each quarter. At the top of the government, Hahua Incas (appointed nobles) reported to Capac Incas (born nobles) who, in turn, reported to the Sapa Inca. The Inca government system was thus like a pyramid with peasants forming the foundation and the Sapa Inca at the very top.

THE SAPA INCA

There were three basic pyramids of power—civil, military, and religious—in the Inca Empire. The Sapa Inca was at the head of all three. He guided the civil government, commanded the military, and was thought to be the direct descendant of the primary Inca god, Inti.

Kings and emperors have always been known by a number of different titles, and this is also true for Inca rulers. First, there was the title Sapa Inca, which means "unique leader." He was also the commander in chief of the army. The people believed he was the "son of the sun," which meant he was a god himself. Finally, the Sapa Inca was also called "lover of the poor" because it was ultimately his responsibility to keep the peasants safe, make sure they had food and clothing, and provide for them in sickness and old age.

It was traditional for the Sapa Inca to take one of his full-blood sisters as his primary wife, or *coya*—although this was not always the case. He was also entitled to take as many secondary wives as he wanted. Some historians claim that some Inca leaders had as many as 100 secondary wives. The secondary wives were often the daughters of high-ranking leaders of conquered peoples or daughters of provincial governors or *apus*. Secondary wives were considered noble but they were not royal. Their children would never lead the empire but would become part of the Inca administration.

The people proved their loyalty to the Sapa Inca in many ways, but the most dramatic was the sacrifice shown by the *capacochas*. In an annual event, the *capacochas*, usually children, were killed as a special sacrifice. Gary Urton, an anthropologist and historian, says in his book, *Inca Myths*, that "These individuals were sent from the provinces to Cuzco where they were sanctified [made holy] by the priests of the Incas. The *capacochas* were then returned to their home territories, marching in sacred procession along straight lines, where they were sacrificed . . . . [T]he sacrifices sealed bonds of alliance between the home community and the Inca in Cuzco."

The Sapa Inca lived an extraordinarily luxurious life, particularly compared to the sunrise-to-sunset workdays of his people. He wore a tunic of the softest vicuña wool and decorated his arms with gold bracelets. Around his neck hung a chest plate of gold and jewels representing the sun. Gold ear plugs three inches in diameter filled his extended earlobes. Even the sandals on his feet were made of gold. Walking in gold sandals may have been a problem, but the Sapa Inca rarely walked; he rode in a litter covered with gold and gems.

The Sapa Inca's days included daily government audiences, where people came to honor him. According to Spanish Cronista Pedro de Cieza de León in *Chronicle of Peru*, "From many of the lords of the country there came emissaries every day bringing gifts; the court was filled with nobles, and his palaces with vessels of gold and silver and other great treasures. In the morning, he took his meal, and from noon until late in the day he gave audience, accompanied by his guard, to whoever wished to talk with him."

Like his subjects, the Sapa Inca ate only two meals a day. While he ate a wider variety of better quality foods, his main meals consisted of similar foods to those the peasants ate. These included potatoes, corn, quinoa, dried llama meat, dried fish, stewed guinea pig, and herbs. The Sapa Inca drank *chicha*, a corn-based beer, just like his subjects. The Inca people rarely drank water (as there was no drinkable water available) or llama milk and they did not have wine.

Beyond the basic laws that Inca subjects lived by, the Sapa Inca could add new laws that suited his particular needs. For example, Cronista Garcilaso de la Vega says in *The Incas* that Sapa Inca Pacha-

Big Ears

When the Spanish arrived in the Inca Empire, they called noble males *orejones*, or "big ears." It was the practice of Inca men to begin wearing earplugs when they reached puberty. Earplugs are disks that fill holes pierced into the earlobe. They are like pierced earrings, but do not hang down. The hole in the earlobe was stretched over the years to hold larger and larger earplugs.

chuti "prohibited any one, except princes and their sons, from wearing gold, silver, precious stones, plumes of feathers of different colors, nor the wool of the vicuña."

THE *COYA*

The *coya* was the Sapa Inca's principal wife, often his full-blooded sister, and mother of the heir to the throne. The *coya* maintained her own household and court, complete with ladies-in-waiting. The grounds around her palace often featured a small botanical garden and a modest zoo.

While the Sapa Inca was the "son of the sun," the *coya* was in charge of the cult of the moon. Commoners often called the *coya* by the title *mamanchic*, which means "our mother" in Quechua, the Inca language.

The *coya* dressed in long robes of soft vicuña wool, gathered at the shoulder with a decorative pin. Servants carried a feathered canopy over her as she walked on a carpet made of fine wool. Her meals, like that of the Sapa Inca, were served on gold and silver plates, although the food was the same eaten by all Inca subjects.

She had no direct ability to rule and could never become Sapa Inca, but she did have general authority over the women of the empire. She also influenced daily politics through her family ties in other royal lines.

Some *coyas* played greater roles in the Inca Empire than others. The most influential may have been the wife of Mayta Capac, Mama Cuca. Botany, landscaping, and other natural sciences fascinated her. After studying agronomy (a branch of

---

IN THEIR OWN WORDS

All in the Family

The idea of a man marrying his own sister may seem shocking, but the Incas were not the only culture that practiced this custom. It was also the practice among the royal family of ancient Egypt and native Hawaii, for example. In his book *The Incas: The Royal Commentaries of the Inca*, Cronista Garcilaso de la Vega explains why the Incas believed this was an important custom:

The law ordaining that the Inca king should marry his eldest sister, born in wedlock, was always respected, and the first-born [son] of this union had the right of succession to his father, on the latter's death. The origin of this law came from the Sun, of which they said that the Moon was both its sister and its bride, and from the first Inca who, according to tradition, was the brother of his bride Mama Occlo.

(Source: de la Vega, Garcilaso. *The Incas: The Royal Commentaries of the Inca, Garcilaso de la Vega*. Translated by Maria Jolas from the critical, annotated edition of Alain Gheerbrant. New York: The Orion Press, 1961.)

agriculture dealing with soil management and crop production), she experimented and introduced new strains of vegetables for farmers. She arranged plantings around the palaces.

Mama Cuca also recognized the value of fishing to provide food and promoted successful fishing techniques among the citizens of the empire. To help the military, she found ways of taking venom from snakes and using the poison to coat arrowheads and spearheads.

Secondary wives could not become the principal wife of the Sapa Inca if the *coya* died. This rule kept the *coya* and her children safe from jealous and ambitious secondary wives—for the most part. Clearly, the policy did not work in the case of Sapa Inca Capac Yupanqui's *coya*, Cusi Hilpay. A secondary wife, Cusi Chimbo, arranged for both the Sapa Inca and the crown prince to be murdered so that Inca Roca, her own son, could be named the new ruler. Chimbo then married Inca Roca and became the *coya* through her second marriage.

This drawing, possibly by missionary Felipe Guaman Poma de Ayala, shows an Inca *coya* in procession with her servants.

CAPAC INCAS AND HAHUA INCAS

Sons and daughters of the Sapa Inca and his many wives were considered nobles. Although only the son of a *coya* could become a Sapa Inca, the other sons had defined roles in society as military leaders, governors, *apus* (regional heads), priests, and administrators.

The various sons, including the heir, went to the school in Cuzco near the royal palace. Schoolboys who had not reached maturity and passed through the Inca puberty rites were called *awkis*. After puberty, they became Incas, which referred to their position as noble men or leaders.

The Sapa Inca's daughters were destined to marry other nobles, be ladies-in-waiting to the *coya*, or enter the Acllahuasi, which housed

Royal Weddings

Marriage among the nobles was serious business, especially those in the extended family of the Sapa Inca. Cronista Garcilaso de la Vega described (in *The Incas: Royal Commentaries)* how these special marriages were sealed by the Sapa Inca himself:

> Every year, or every two years, the Inca gathered together in Cuzco all the young people of his line, both girls and boys, who were at an age to be married. The girls had to be between 18 and 20 years old, and the boys had to have celebrated their 24th birthdays. They were forbidden to marry at an earlier age. The Inca took his place among them, then, having looked attentively at them, he joined them together, two by two, and returned them like this to their parents, who led them to the house of the young man's father, where the marriage was celebrated a few days later. The women chosen in this way were the legitimate wives referred to in their language as the wife received from the hand of the king.

(Source: de la Vega, Garcilaso. *The Incas: The Royal Commentaries of the Inca, Garcilaso de la Vega.* Translated by Maria Jolas from the critical, annotated edition of Alain Gheerbrant. New York: The Orion Press, 1961.)

holy, or chosen women. As unmarried women, the princesses were called *nyostas.* Once married, they were called *palyas.*

A noble-born Inca was a person who could trace his family tree back to Manco Capac, the first Sapa Inca, however remotely. These nobles had the title Capac Inca, which means "capable leader." They were also relatives of the Sapa Inca, although they could be distant cousins.

Direct descendants of Manco Capac could be part of the state council, which is much like the president's cabinet in the United States. These men advised the Sapa Inca on the state of the empire and made sure orders given by the Sapa Inca were carried out. Four Capac Incas ran the four quarters of the empire as *apus.*

Hahua Incas were appointed to the noble class and rose in status by showing devotion to the Sapa Inca or through outstanding military service. Like the Capac Incas, they did the brainwork of running the empire. They planned, organized, supervised, and managed large groups of citizens.

Nobles received gifts and privileges from the Sapa Inca, including tunics of *cumbi* (vicuña wool), which they might wear for special occasions in Cuzco. They also gained land, servants, herds of llamas, and wives selected for them by the Sapa Inca. Polygamy (having more than one wife) was a right only of the noble classes.

Capac Incas and Hahua Incas rode in litters and used gold or silver bowls or plates. Most importantly, they did not have to pay regular taxes to the Sapa Inca and the religious sector.

CURACAS AND OTHER CIVIL LEADERS

Curacas came from the lower ranks of the nobles and from former leaders of conquered cultures. *Curacas* were part of the Inca government system, overseeing large groups of households, usually 100, 500, 1,000, or 5,000 in number. The primary functions of *curacas* were to make sure workers worked and taxpayers paid taxes.

Curacas had some of the same rights as nobles. They received gifts of land, servants, and cloth from the Sapa Inca and could ride in litters and have more than one wife. Higher level *curacas* also did not have to pay taxes.

Curacas had to prove their loyalty to the Sapa Inca and perform their jobs without favoritism or corruption. They were expected to spend part of their time in Cuzco, waiting on the Sapa Inca while their sons attended school in the capital. Daughters might be married as secondary wives to the Sapa Inca, Capac Incas, or Hahua Incas.

Beneath the level of *curaca* was the *camayoc*, or foreman, who served as local leader of an *ayllu*. The *camayoc* kept track of the work and production of people within his group. The positions of *curaca* and *camayoc* were both inherited, and fathers trained their sons in their future careers.

NEITHER NOBLE NOR COMMON

Artisans, engineers, architects, and other skilled workers fell somewhere between the nobles and the peasants. The Chimú, for example (conquered by the Inca around 1465) were excellent jewelers, goldsmiths, and silversmiths. The Inca honored these talents. Although these people were not required to work in the fields, they were expected to contribute two-thirds of whatever they made to the Sapa Inca and the religious community.

Stonemasons, architects, and engineers worked for the Sapa Inca. Although they did not produce items that could be sold or traded, their services were highly valued. Because these services benefited the community as a whole and the Sapa Inca in particular, architects and engineers were not required to perform other labors or to pay taxes.

COMMONERS

Peasants lived their lives under a strict code of rules. They could be farmers, herders, miners, or fishermen. But they did not get to choose. A boy had to follow the same profession as his father.

Government officials watched over their work and provided for them if crops failed, they got sick or injured, or they reached the Inca retirement age of 50 years old. Retirement was not a matter of sleeping late and relaxing, though. Older people still worked. They just did not build roads, plow fields, serve in the army, or dig in the mines.

Everyone worked to the best of their abilities—even children and the elderly. However, those who were unable to work were fed, housed, and clothed at the Sapa Inca's expense. Today, this type of system would be called a socialist government.

The lives of peasants were as structured as everything else in the Inca Empire. The government planned for every stage of life. If conquered people had too much free time, the Inca rulers believed they might become restless. Absolute control was also necessary because there were never more than about 1,000 Incas ruling a region that covered five modern countries and that was populated by dozens of different ethnic groups and millions of people.

Once a child reached five years old, he or she had jobs. Girls learned to cut kernels from corncobs, dehydrate potatoes, and cook. Boys carried water, kept away pests from crops, and helped with planting and harvesting. Older girls watched over their younger brothers and sisters, fetched water and food for livestock, cooked meals, and weeded fields.

Once girls reached 16 to 20 years old, they were married. Wives maintained the house, helped with plowing and planting, processed and stored food, and had children. Young men married at about age 25 and were immediately enrolled as taxpayers. District governors arranged marriages for people who did not choose spouses on their own. Living as a single man or woman was not acceptable.

Formal education was not available to children of peasants or craftspeople. The children learned from their parents.

This gold figurine, wrapped in multicolored woven cloth fastened with a gold pin, is an Inca depiction of a chosen woman. Selection as a chosen woman offered upward social mobility for a girl.

The two areas in which there was some possibility to get ahead were the military and the religious community. A young man who showed exceptional skills as a warrior might rise to lead a troop of 10, a battalion of 50 or 100, or become commander of a regiment.

In the religious community, attractive girls around 10 years old might be selected to become one of the chosen women, or *acllas*. These girls studied at the Acllahuasi, where they learned expert weaving skills, made *chicha* for the Sapa Inca and the priests, and participated in religious rites. Some girls would become brides of nobles or secondary wives of the Sapa Inca. Others remained in the religious life, eventually becoming teachers in the Acllahuasi. Some became *capacochas*— human sacrifices.

MITMAKONAS

On occasion, a newly conquered group of people did not fit in well with the structure of the Inca Empire. The solution to this problem was to break up rebellious groups and send the people to work somewhere else, where the people were loyal to the empire. Their departure left a messy gap in the workforce. The Inca government filled this gap with *mitmakonas*.

Mitmakonas were people loyal to the Sapa Inca, people who followed the pattern of hard work and paying taxes. They moved to the rebellious region and brought order by setting a good example. Entire families, *ayllus*, or several *ayllus* were moved into the region.

It was an honor to be chosen to be a *mitmakona*, both for the individual and the community. *Mitmakonas* received special privileges, including wearing their "home colors"—the dress and headgear of their particular regions—even while living in their new location. In their new locations, the *mitmakonas* could also follow the ethnic and religious customs of their home regions.

The tribal or ethnic community from which *mitmakonas* came also benefited, since they might be given additional land for crops or other privileges. In her book, *Kingdom of the Sun*, historian Ruth Karen writes, "A loyal highland people that had furnished an appreciable number of *mitmakona* might be awarded fields in the lowlands, which its *purics* (taxpayers) could work to obtain products—fruit and vegetables that could not be grown in their own, colder climate." Of course, those new products were taxed at the normal rate: one-third to the community, two-thirds to the Sapa Inca and the religious community.

TAXES

Workers paid two-thirds of everything they produced in taxes. For example, farmers paid their taxes by working the fields and pastures owned by the government. One-third of the crop was the *ayllu's* to keep. Another third, placed in storehouses for distribution in case of drought or famine, was the property of the Sapa Inca. The last third belonged to the priests and religious groups, and was used to feed the people at religious events and for sacrifices to the gods. Other occupations paid tax in a similar way, keeping only one-third of their production.

The Incas did not use currency of any kind. Instead, they used a system of trading called the barter system, in which objects of equal value were traded. Among the most highly valued products was cloth. Every woman spun cotton or wool into thread and wove cloth in her

---

IN THEIR OWN WORDS

Everyone Pays Taxes

Since the Incas did not have currency, taxes were paid in products. Cronista Garcilaso de la Vega explained the wide variety of items the Inca people used to pay their taxes in his book, *The Incas: Royal Commentaries*:

> In the richer provinces, shoes were made out of a vegetable raw material derived from agave plants. In the same way, weapons came from different regions, according to the various materials that entered into their making. One province furnished bows and arrows, and another lances, javelins, hatchets, and bludgeons . . . .
>
> Thus, the Inca's vassals [subordinates] furnished him with four types of statute labor: they tilled his land, spun and wove his wool and cotton, and manufactured shoes and weapons for his troops.
>
> We shall add to these the special tribute that, every year, the poor and disinherited paid to the governors of the territory that they lived in; which consisted of a tube filled with lice.
>
> The Incas said that this token tribute was intended to show that everyone, no matter what his station owed something to the State, in exchange for the benefits he received from it.

(Source: de la Vega, Garcilaso. *The Incas: The Royal Commentaries of the Inca, Garcilaso de la Vega*. Translated by Maria Jolas from the critical, annotated edition of Alain Gheerbrant. New York: The Orion Press, 1961.)

free time. Cloth could also be used to pay taxes. It was stored in government warehouses for clothing the poor or the military.

In addition to a share of crops or goods produced, all adult males had to provide a period of labor, called *mit'a*, to the government. A farmer, for example, might provide two weeks of service in the army, building roads, or digging in the mines. While he was gone, the other members of his *ayllu* worked his fields and made sure his family was fed. Often, if the *mit'a* duty was mining or construction, the worker could bring along his wife and family. Through the *mit'a*, the Incas built paved roads, canals, bridges, and agricultural terraces. *Mit'a* labor supported irrigation programs, dug gold and silver from mines, and built government storehouses.

KEEPING ACCURATE ACCOUNTS

Because the Incas had no written language, they developed a system of accounting or recording that mathematicians today still have trouble figuring out. This system was *quipu*, which means "knots." The government depended on the accuracy of the *quipu* at every level.

A *quipu* might be a few inches long or as much as 10 feet, with thousands of strings. Here is an example of how a *quipu* might be constructed: The *quipu*-maker counts herds and crop yields in a region to decide how much tax the people must pay. There are 100 taxable households, and their products include 25 herds of llamas and a variety of farm crops. The first set of knots, perhaps in brown yarn, might show one big knot for the 100 households, followed by sets of smaller knots, loops, and twists to show the breakdown of these 100 households by the number of children each had. They might show 42 households with three children, 36 with two children, 14 with one child, and eight with no children. The next set of knots, possibly white, might indicate 25 herds of llamas with connected knots showing the number of animals per herd, and so on. Crops might be listed in

Each *quipu*-maker developed his own system of colors and knots. This is Felipe Guaman Poma de Ayala's drawing from *La nueva crónica y buen gobierno*.

CÖTADOR·MAIOR·ITEZORERO
TAVANTIN·SVIO·QVIPO
CVRACA·CON DOR·CHAVA

size order: corn, potatoes, quinoa, and so on, with each crop having a specific color of string.

The *quipu*-maker (called *quipu camayocs*) recorded the number of taxpayers in a region, an accurate count of the population, the amount and variety of crops grown or products produced, and the tax paid for every bit of material grown, dug, or created. Several *quipu*-makers might be charged with recording the same territory (as a kind of backup system). Those at higher levels made *quipus* incorporating data from several smaller *ayllus*.

The problem in understanding the system today is that every *quipu*-maker used different colors, knot formations, and arrangements of strings to make his *quipu*. Only the person who made the *quipu* could translate its meaning.

Cronistas of the Inca Empire (the Spanish soldiers, clerks, and priests who wrote detailed accounts of the history, customs, and daily lives of the Inca citizens) wrote about *quipus* and *quipu*-makers. Every quarter, province, and district had several *quipu*-makers who were constantly recording every detail of Inca life, so archaeologists might expect to find many *quipus* in burial sites. But few *quipus* still exist. That is because Spanish priests believed *quipus* were pagan items that needed to be destroyed. They burned thousands of records that might have provided a key to understanding the *quipu*.

Only about 400 *quipus* remain in existence, and they were found in burial mounds. Based on the evidence of several burials, the archaeologists believe that bodies buried with *quipus* were possibly important people of the district.

The first hint of what the *quipus* meant was unraveled by L. Leland Locke of New York's American Museum of Natural History in 1910. Mathematicians continue to study *quipus*, making slow progress in understanding the accounting system of a culture that had no written language.

THE LAW

With social and civil structures so clearly defined, there were few laws in the Inca Empire. The basic laws were:

◈ Do not be lazy.
◈ Do not lie.

◆ Do not steal.

◆ Do not commit murder.

◆ Do not commit adultery (cheat on your spouse).

These laws were strictly enforced. People of higher social status who committed crimes were punished much more severely than commoners were. The Incas believed a better lifestyle demanded better behavior.

Breaking the law was not acceptable, and punishments could be dreadful. The most gruesome was, perhaps, being hung over a deep ravine by the hair. When the hair roots gave out, the victim fell to certain death on the rocks below.

Says Michael Malpass in his book, *Daily Life in the Inca Empire*, "Adultery among commoners was punishable by torture; but if the woman was a noble, both parties were executed. Crimes against the government were treated with special severity. Stealing from the fields of the state was punishable by death. If a *curaca* put a person to death without permission of his superior, a [heavy] stone was dropped on his back from a height of three feet. If he did it again, he was killed. Treason was punished by imprisoning the person in an underground prison in Cuzco that was filled with snakes and dangerous animals."

District officials acted as judges, holding trials for the crimes committed in their regions. Crime at any social level was rare, since the guilty person was sure to be caught and punishment was swift and harsh. Trials usually took place within five days of the criminal being caught, and sentences were carried out immediately.

Death sentences were common for murder, adultery with a noble, and theft of property from the Sapa Inca or the religious warehouses. Commoners were beaten to death with stone clubs or thrown over the side of a cliff. The punishment of having a heavy stone dropped from a three-foot height might bring death or serious injury.

The punishment of being jailed in the "Place of the Pit" was a death sentence reserved for nobles and government leaders. The pit was a maze filled with poisonous snakes, spiders, scorpions, and hungry pumas. The walls and floor had jagged rocks and metal shards embedded in them, so the prisoners could find no rest. Of course, water and food were not provided.

A starving person who stole food received a lesser punishment than a person who stole food he did not need to keep himself and his family alive. The local government administrator in that person's district was punished even more harshly. Under Inca rule, no one was expected to go hungry. Thus, a starving person showed that the local administrator was not doing his job. His punishment could be loss of rank, public insult, or, in serious situations, banishment to the coca fields on the eastern slope of the Andes.

For commoners, the code of life was, *Ama sua, ama llulla, ama checklla* (Do not steal, lie, or be lazy). A lazy woman who kept a dirty home was forced to eat her own household dirt. Her husband, also held responsible for a poorly kept home, had to eat dirt or drink the waste water left after his dirty family bathed. A lazy field worker might be tortured or whipped for failing to work, and repeated laziness meant a death sentence by clubbing.

Even marriage had its set of regulations, overseen by civil government officials. The Incas did not believe in divorce or separation. Marriage lasted a lifetime. If a husband tried to get rid of his wife, he was forced to take her back. A second offense meant public punishment for the husband. Putting out his wife three times meant death for the husband by clubbing or being thrown off a cliff.

Marriage laws applied to all citizens. Nobles were allowed to put out a secondary wife, but they had to keep their primary wife for life.

Such punishments were rare because crime was rare. Since the standard punish-

CONNECTIONS

Coca!

Under Inca rule, only nobles grew and possessed coca. They could and did give it to commoners at celebrations or to people who were not used to working at high altitudes. The coca was chewed, releasing stimulating drugs into the saliva that relieved many aches and pains.

Today, Andean people still rely on coca leaves in religious rituals and as a folk medicine. The leaves are offered as part of a gift to ancient gods and are "read" by fortunetellers who claim to see the future. More importantly, coca serves as an herbal medicine in a region where doctors are scarce. Coca is brewed in tea to relieve headaches and dizzy spells and to heal sore throats and upset stomachs. The tea helps people suffering from altitude sickness. Herbal healers make poultices (medicated masses placed on sores or wounds) to put on achy joints or bone injuries.

Coca is also the plant from which drug dealers make cocaine. Coca plants grown in Peru fall under the control of the government, and the Coca National Enterprise sells the leaves for herbal use and the manufacture of prescription drugs. Unfortunately, small farmers also grow coca for illegal sale, because one year's cocaine crop can be sold for enough money to feed, clothe, and house a large family for a year. One year's corn crop, on the other hand, does not feed the family for a full winter.

ment for most crimes was a painful death, few people committed any crimes. Even fewer committed more than one crime. Inca citizens learned from birth that their lot in life was work, work, work. They expected nothing else, so they rarely rebelled against the government's expectations.

TRADE AND TRANSPORT

The Incas did not trade with their neighbors. If a culture had something the Incas wanted or needed, they conquered the people. Because the empire became so large, the Inca Empire needed nothing that it did not have. But trade within the empire was brisk. All trading was on the barter system—trading goods or services for items considered by both parties to be of equal value. The Incas had no form of currency.

Inca communities produced a variety of food for the empire: corn and potatoes, quinoa, dried llama or fish, herbs, peppers, and hundreds

CONNECTIONS

A Life on the Reeds

At 12,580 feet above sea level, Lake Titicaca is the world's highest lake that can be navigated by boat. For centuries, the people of the region have raised potatoes on the surrounding land and fished the icy lake waters. The boats used for fishing today are nearly identical in design and size to boats used in Inca times. The boats are made of reeds carefully tied into bundles. They slip across the water, powered by sails made of woven reeds or by sturdy poles in the shallows.

The totora reed has been the foundation of local life for more than 1,000 years. The local people live on a series of floating reed islands in the lake known as the Uros Islands. They use the totora reed to build houses and

A Quechua family navigates Lake Titicaca in a reed canoe.

boats, and to support the base of their island homes. No part of the totora reed goes to waste, and even the roots can be roasted or boiled for a meal.

of other foods. Different regions may have eaten different foods, but hunger was rare. Mountain people ate more guinea pig and llama meat; coastal groups ate fish and seafood.

Trading within the empire took place at regional markets. People traded cloth for llama skins, dried llama meat for dried fish, pottery for medicinal herbs, and so on. For example, if a woman with a sore eye needed medical care, she might pay four potatoes or a length of cloth for treatment by the local herbalist.

One factor that limited trade was a lack of transportation. The Incas did not have the wheel, so carts were not a transportation option. They did not have horses or oxen to bear heavy loads. Humans or llamas carried goods on their backs.

The Incas did have boats and rafts, but they were usually used for short-distance travel or for fishing. Rafts on mountain rivers and lakes were made of reeds and, occasionally logs, but they were not strong enough to carry heavy loads. Along the Pacific Ocean, larger ocean-going rafts, built from logs and sealskins, carried fishermen out to sea. They, too, did not carry heavy loads. They also were not strong enough to travel over great distances.

CHAPTER 5

LIVING AMONG THE INCAS

LAZINESS WAS A CRIME IN THE INCA EMPIRE, SO WORK dominated daily life. Inca subjects lived by two calendars: one diurnal (daytime) and the other nocturnal (nighttime). The diurnal calendar was based on the movements of the sun and was 365 days long. It set the work pattern for the empire, including specific agricultural activities, building projects, and warfare. The nocturnal calendar was based on the movements of the moon and was 328 nights long. It determined the schedule of rituals and religious celebrations.

The fact that the two calendars did not have an equal number of days did not bother the Incas. What happened on nights that were not on the calendar is not known.

Because the Inca Empire lay close to the equator, there were not four true seasons. The climate had only wet and dry seasons. However, the altitude in many Inca regions was so high that snow, ice, and blizzards were common.

December (Capac Raymi) started each new year. It was the time for planting coca, some types of potatoes, and quinoa. At night, the people celebrated puberty rituals for boys reaching manhood. During this month, taxes, sacrifices, and gifts to the Sapa Inca arrived in Cuzco.

January (Camay Quilla) saw farmers preparing their fields. Men and women worked side by side with wooden ploughs and hoes. The nocturnal calendar continued puberty ceremonies, often spanning three weeks or more.

February (Hatun Pucuy) and March (Pacha Pucuy) were considered late summer. There were harvests of potatoes, jicama, and other root vegetables. At night, rituals and sacrifices were made to improve corn and grain crop yields.

April (Ayrihua) found peasants chasing away deer, foxes, and birds from the cornfields to stop them from eating crops. Farmers pounded loud drums and hurled pebbles with their slingshots at hungry birds to protect crops as they ripened for harvest. At night, commoners took part in ceremonies to honor their leader, the Sapa Inca.

May (Aymoray Quilla) brought the corn harvest and celebrations much like the Thanksgiving holiday celebrated in the United States today.

June (Inti Raymi) celebrated the Inca sun god each evening. The days were spent harvesting more potatoes and tubers (root vegetables), and other crops.

July (Chahua Harquiz) was the heart of the Inca winter. However, work continued despite the cold and sometimes even snow. Meats were smoked or dried, potatoes were freeze-dried for storage. Men served their *mit'as* by building and repairing irrigation ditches and canals. Religious rituals were offered in honor of irrigation, since most of the crops eaten by the people of the Inca Empire depended on irrigation systems. It was only natural for the people to ask their gods to bless the systems that carried life-giving water to their fields.

August (Yapaquiz) and September (Coya Raymi) were the spring-like planting season. Farmers used foot hoes to turn the winter-hardened soil, planting corn seeds and early potato crops. Grains and other crops were planted after the corn and potato crops were secure. Religious rites during this season ensured the help of the Inca gods in providing good crops and controlling the negative elements of nature. During Coya Raymi, rites were also offered to cleanse and purify the capital city of Cuzco.

October (K'antaray) and November (Ayamarca) were dedicated to promoting good crops, as the people prayed for rain—but not too much. Historically, Ayamarca saw little rain, and farmers began using irrigation ditches to water the corn crops. This season honored the dead at a festival where mummies of earlier Sapa Incas were brought from their homes on golden litters and offered gifts of gold, cloth, and food.

FROM BIRTH TO OLD AGE

Birth was nothing special and no cause for celebration. Mothers gave birth on their own. While a mother was in labor the father did not eat, and this was believed to ensure a healthy birth. Immediately after birth, the mother washed her newborn in cold water from a nearby stream.

The newborn child was called *wawa*, or baby, and was not named for at least a year. A few days after birth, the infant was placed in a *quirau*, or cradle, similar to a papoose board in Native North American cultures. Babies were kept tightly strapped in the *quirau* throughout the day.

When old enough to crawl or stand, the baby would be placed in a hole in the ground that was deep enough to keep the child from harm during the day. This allowed mother to work while the baby fended for itself. Babies were breastfed but never held or cuddled. Cronista Garcilaso de la Vega described Inca mothers in his book, *The Incas: Royal Commentaries:*

> *Neither in giving them milk, nor at any other time, did they ever take them in their arms, for they said that this would make them cry, and want always to be in their mothers' arms and never in their cradles. The mother leant over her child and gave it the breast, and this was done three times a day . . . . They did not give the child milk at any other time, even if it cried, for they said that if they did it would want to be sucking all day long, and become dirty with vomitings, and that when it was a man it would grow up a great eater and a glutton.*

Mothers did not stop breastfeeding their children until they were a year old or more. At this point, the family and friends celebrated a ceremony called *rutuchicoy*, when a close uncle or grandfather would be first to cut a lock from the child's hair. Other guests cut locks of hair and gave the child or family gifts. At this time, the child received a temporary name that usually reflected events surrounding the birth. A boy might be named Hawk, Snake, or Flood. A girl might be called Silver, Gold, or Sunshine. Temporary names were used until a child reached puberty.

By six years old, children were expected to work. Boys and girls chased animals from crop fields, collected fruit and nuts, and helped with household chores. Girls learned to spin thread, weave cloth, and prepare food. Boys learned how to make sandals of grass, wool, or leather, how to plow, dig in the mines, cut rock—whatever their future jobs would be. Although children did not do as much work as an

CONNECTIONS

The First Haircut

The *rutuchicoy*, or first haircut, was an important ceremony in Inca life that took place when a child was about one year old. It remains an honored tradition among today's Andes people, although the event now takes place when the child is about three to five years old. Friends and family gather around to assist in the haircut and the party afterward. This usually includes a lot of *chicha* (beer), food, and music. The child sits in the place of honor as each adult cuts a lock of hair from his or her head. Guests present the child with gifts. Money given at the *rutuchicoy* forms the basis of a savings account for later life.

adult, they learned from birth that play came second to hard work and laziness was never acceptable.

Inca boys became men at roughly 14 years of age. The event was celebrated by the entire community at feast held during Capac Raymi (December). The feast, called *huarachicoy*, lasted several weeks and featured massive meals, dances, and tests of strength and endurance. Boys received their first loincloth (a single piece of cloth worn wrapped around the hips), woven by their mothers, along with other clothing worn by adults. They also received their first weapons of war: a slingshot, a shield, and a mace. These represented a man's ability to serve in the military.

The *huarachicoy* included a trip by the boys to Huanacauri, a sacred mountain near Cuzo. Each boy brought a llama to be sacrificed to the spirit of the mountain. As they returned down the mountain, their relatives whipped their legs with sticks. The boys were expected to endure the pain without whining to show that they had reached manhood. Once past the puberty ceremony, teenage boys took on greater responsibility, although they still did not carry a full adult workload until they got married.

Puberty rituals for girls were a minor event compared to those for boys. The puberty ceremony for girls took place when the girl had her first menstrual period. The family and friends then celebrated for two days at an event called *quicochicoy*. A girl fasted (ate nothing) for three days. On the fourth day, she appeared before her friends and family freshly bathed and dressed in fine clothing.

For both boys and girls, puberty was the time when they received permanent or adult names. These rituals were performed for every social class. However, only noble boys underwent the ceremony of ear piercing. As they matured, young men's earlobes would stretch more and more until they could wear golden earplugs measuring up to three inches across.

Inca men married at about age 25 and girls married between ages 16 and 20. Men and women of marriageable age could choose their own mates, have marriages arranged for them by their families, or have a government-negotiated marriage. The local *curaca*, or leader, had to approve any marriage, and regional governors performed the actual marriage ceremony.

Members of the couple's *ayllu*, or local clan, built a one-room house for the couple. Their parents provided household goods, including cooking pots, bowls, baskets, and blankets.

When the governor recorded the marriage, the husband automatically became a *puric*, or taxpayer. The Sapa Inca provided each *puric* with enough land to support the husband and wife, although the amount of land depended on the region and its ability to produce crops. This parcel of land, called the *topo*, might be one or two acres. The couple didn't actually own the land, because the government owned all land in the Inca Empire. They were just granted the right to farm on the land.

As a couple had children, they received additional land. The birth of each son might entitle the couple to another acre or two; each daughter, one-half acre.

Marriage for members of the nobility was very different from marriage among commoners. Men of the noble class practiced polygamy (taking two or more wives), but Inca law forbid polygamy among commoners.

Inheritance and succession (passing on the family's rank) was based on both a child's mother and father. The father had to be a member of the noble class, but only the children of his primary wife were also nobles. Children of secondary wives filled the growing need for regional rulers. If a primary wife died, a secondary wife could not take her place. This practice reduced jealousy and probably saved the lives of many primary wives and their sons.

People who were too old, too sick, or too disabled to work were supported by the government. Few people lived to age 50, but anyone who did retired from the normal adult workload. They were given tasks suited to their age, such as stripping corn from the cob, drying or smoking fish or meat, or educating children about household chores.

Widows were not required to marry again, and a farmer's widow kept the family *topo* until she died. The members of her *ayllu* plowed and planted it for her. If she was still able to work, she might assist in the planting, weeding, or harvesting. However, she was not expected to farm the land without help.

RURAL LIFE

The Inca love for order and organization extended to the most remote areas of the empire. Rural folk worked at various jobs, such as farming, herding, and mining. Depending on the altitude and irrigation system, farmers grew corn, various types of potatoes, beans, squash, fruit, and dozens of other food plants and herbs.

Men and women worked the fields together. The man turned the soil with a foot plow, called a *taclla*, while his wife moved along the plowed row, breaking up soil clumps with a *lampa*, a wooden hoe.

Those who worked with livestock maintained herds of llamas that provided food, wool, leather, and pack animals. A llama could travel about 20 miles a day. Greater distances were not possible, because llama

Llamas have been used for centuries as pack animals throughout Peru.

handlers walked beside their animals.

Most mines were high in the Andes Mountains, where work was difficult because the high altitude meant reduced oxygen levels and colder temperatures. Most miners did not work a full Inca workday of sunrise to sunset. Instead, they usually worked only six to eight hours in the mines.

Men were responsible for doing their daily jobs, hunting under the watchful eye of the local *camayoc* (leader), paying taxes, and serving their *mit'a*. They provided labor for repairing or building roads, irrigation canals, and bridges, and could be called on to serve in the military. Men also made their family's sandals, either from woven plant fibers, wool, or leather, along with pottery, weapons, and wooden tools. Even the Sapa Inca knew how to make sandals—a skill required of every adult male.

CONNECTIONS

Llama Jerky?

Inca wives were experts at preserving llama meat to make *charqui*. This meat product, pronounced *CHAR-kee*, is sold today in convenience stores and supermarkets throughout the United States as jerky (although in the United States it is usually made from beef).

Traditional *charqui* (unlike modern jerky) consisted of seasoned and dehydrated meat packages that included bones. The Incas used the cold, dry conditions of high altitudes to accomplish the dehydration.

Charqui preserved meat for storage in government and religious warehouses and fed families during the long Andes Mountain winters. Pieces of the meat were added to potatoes, other tubers (root vegetables), or dried corn to make wholesome stews.

Traditional style llama *charqui* is still sold today in Peru's open-air markets. It remains a basic source of protein for many people who live in the Andes.

Women worked the fields, cooked, raised the children, nursed the sick, and kept house. They spun fiber into yarn and wove cloth to provide clothing for the family and to pay taxes. There was no time wasted in a woman's day. Any idle time, including walking to and from the fields, was spent spinning and weaving.

Rural children received no formal schooling. Instead, they learned their future jobs from their parents. Since there was no opportunity to move up in society, they needed no other education.

Families lived in one-room houses with stonewalls and roofs made of bundles of straw or grass called thatch. Since there was little theft—and most people owned nothing of great value—houses did not have doors or windows, just open entryways. Houses offered protection from the elements at night, when families huddled together on piles of straw to sleep. Eating, cooking, general work, childcare, and all other daily chores were done outside, regardless of the weather.

CITY LIFE

On special occasions, such as paying taxes or taking part in religious celebrations, government administrators and subjects headed to the Inca cities. Cuzco was the Inca capital, but each region had at least one major city where government officials lived and religious ceremonies took place.

At a time when European cities had open sewers and garbage was dumped into the streets, Inca cities had clean running water and a complex sewer system. Some city engineers tapped into underground hot springs to provide nobles with hot and cold running water.

Expert weavers, potters, masons, and metalworkers went to the cities to work. These jobs, like farming and herding, were passed from generation to generation. Children of craftsmen began studying for their trades at about six years old.

Even in the cities, few children attended schools. With no written language and a strict social structure that limited advancement, children had no need to know more than they could learn at home. Formal education was limited to sons of nobles, sons of provincial rulers and conquered leaders, and the chosen women *acllas*.

Noble boys went to the school in Cuzco for about four years, where they learned history and military strategy, religion, and the use and development of the *quipu* record-keeping system. Teachers— *amautas*—disciplined their students by beating or whipping them. This practice was acceptable to Inca parents.

City life was not much different from rural life because people were still expected to work from sunrise to sunset. They used their homes for sleeping and performed all other daily tasks outside.

WHAT THE INCAS ATE

Urban or rural, Sapa Inca, nobleman, farmer, or miner, Inca people all ate roughly the same food. The Sapa Inca ate his meals off gold or silver plates while his people ate off wooden platters. But they all ate corn, potatoes, grains, and meat.

Between 50 and 60 percent of the plants people worldwide eat today can be traced back to the region in which the Incas lived. The two most common and important were corn, or maize, and potatoes. Maize was not a staple anywhere in Peru until after 500 B.C.E. It first appeared about 6000 B.C.E. in Mexico, and from there spread in primitive form through Central America and northern South America. It seems to have arrived in Peru before 3000 B.C.E., but did not become an important crop until much later. Even in among the Chavín people, maize was only a secondary crop. However, in Inca times it was the staple

CONNECTIONS

The World of Potatoes

It would seem that all potatoes are the same. But that is not so. In the Andes Mountains, roughly 3,000 different potato varieties are grown and sold. Lima, Peru, is home to the International Potato Center, where some 5,000 potato species have been developed.

Today, most potatoes around the world are members of one of about seven different potato species. The most common type of potato eaten in the world today is the s*olanum tuberosum*, which is directly traced to Inca agriculture. In fact, the *solanum tuberosum* was one of several hundred potatoes and tubers (root vegetables) grown in the Inca Empire.

The Incas cooked potatoes in stews, baked them in beds of hot coals, and prepared them for storage. The Incas developed *chuño*, the first freeze-dried potatoes—a bit like present-day instant mashed potatoes. The potatoes were sliced thin and placed in neat rows outside, where they froze overnight. Each morning for several days, ice

Villagers cook freshly harvested potatoes in an underground pit during the June Potato Festival in Huancavelia, Peru. The festival is organized by the International Potato Center.

crystals were removed from the potato slices until the potatoes were dry. Freeze-dried potatoes fed Inca families through long winters and famines, and were stored in warehouses for feeding the army or hungry citizens. They were also placed at rest stops along Inca roads to feed travelers on their trips.

throughout the empire. Potatoes were the other staple food in nearly every meal the Incas ate.

The Inca people ate a variety of plant foods, including spices and seasonings, such as hot and chili peppers, and several types of mint. They also ate algae, squash, tomatoes, pumpkins, and palmetto (a type of palm tree). Among fruits and nuts, Incas enjoyed pineapples, sour cherries, custard apples, cashew nuts, cactus fruit, plums, peanuts, elderberries, guavas, avocados, and an ancient form of bananas.

Potatoes and sweet potatoes were common root vegetables, along with jicama, oca, yucca, cassava, ollucu, mashua, and begonia. Beans included kidney beans, lima beans, and string beans, along with uncommon varieties such as cazza, pashuru, and tarwi.

Cereal grains common in Inca times included maize, quinoa, caniwa, and amaranth. Today, people still eat corn on the cob, creamed, popped, and as hominy grits or corn bread. Quinoa and amaranth are popular grains available at health food stores in bread, crackers, breakfast cereal, and flour. Amaranth has been added to the diet of NASA astronauts because of its important nutritional value.

Along with beans, meat provided needed protein for Inca people. The vast majority of meat eaten by people in the Inca empire came from llamas or alpacas. Guinea pigs were party food and were more important as a source of fat than protein. Those who lived along the ocean or major rivers enjoyed tuna, catfish, sardines, king fish, mussels, and clams.

Inca people used dietary supplements, much as people do today. They ate kaolin (a type of clay) for upset stomach or indigestion. Kaolin is a main ingredient in many common medicines people take today for the same problems. Inca cooks added salt and pepper to their foods for flavor and because salt is a dietary necessity. They also ate mineral lime to add calcium for strong bones.

Every household, whether rural or urban, produced a type of beer made from corn and local berries. The beer, called *chicha*, was made in large pottery urns. It was cooled by partially burying the urns in the ground or by placing them in icy cold mountain streams. Inca people outside the cities also drank water from clean mountain springs.

CLOTHING

Cloth was so highly valued by the Incas that it was used as a type of currency, and many people paid taxes or bought needed goods with cloth.

A number of expert weavers—usually men or *acllas*—wove cloth for the Sapa Inca. The finest cloth was made from vicuña wool (wool from a wild relative of the llama) and was kept for use only by the nobles. Gifts of vicuña wool from the Sapa Inca were prized. The *acllas* also produced cloth used for religious shrines, priests, and priestesses.

Clothes for commoners were made of llama wool or a blend of wool and cotton. People living near the coast, where it was hotter, wore light-weight cotton.

Regardless of rank, most men and women wore the same style of clothes. Men wore tunics that reached to the knees and loincloths for undergarments. Women wore long dresses that reached to the ankles and were held in place by a belt tied around the waist. Both men and women wore sandals made of grass or leather that were worn year round, even when it snowed.

RELIGION

While work consumed the diurnal, or daytime, calendar, religion dominated the nocturnal, or nighttime, calendar. Every month had at least one major religious celebration and three or more lesser ones. So the Incas had 120 days of religious rituals throughout the year. Celebrating life events added joy to the heavy workloads of the Inca people, whether they lived in heavily populated urban centers or in remote rural towns.

The Incas believed that the god Viracocha, who was neither male nor female, created the earth, sky, stars, and all living things. They believed Viracocha made the sun and moon by plucking them from an island in Lake Titicaca, high in the Andes

CONNECTIONS

Bring Back the Sun

In the 1940s, citizens of the city of Cuzco decided to revive an ancient ritual, the festival of Inti Raymi. The ceremonies conducted each evening of June banished winter and encouraged the return of the sun and its warmth.

Today, the feast is celebrated on June 24, when city and rural families parade through Cuzco's streets to the fortress ruin of Sacsahuaman, built under Inca ruler Pachacuti (r. 1438–1471). The person selected to be Inca-of-the-day arrives dressed in a mix of shiny foil and cheap clothing. Dancers in beautiful hand-woven outfits twirl beneath the winter skies. The fires that once symbolized Inca rituals blaze for hours, as a llama appears as a symbol of the sacrifice to the gods (this llama is not sacrificed!).

The event serves as the opening ceremonies for a week-long fair that draws people from throughout the Andes and beyond.

Mountains. People and animals were formed from clay in Tiahuanaco on the lakeshore.

The Incas honored the sun, Inti, as an important god, portraying Inti as a face within a golden disk and surrounded by rays. Officially, the Sapa Inca was the "son of the sun," a divine being who descended directly from the sun god. When the Sapa Inca died, the people believed he returned to the sun.

The major religious event of the year was the Inti Raymi, a multi-day festival honoring Inti, complete with food supplied by the Sapa Inca and local priests. Sixteenth-century Catholic priest Cristóbal de Molina described the celebration in *The Fables and Rites of the Incas*: "All the people of Cuzco came out, according to their tribes and lineage, as richly dressed as their means would allow; and having made reverences to the Creator, the Sun, and the lord Inca, they sat down on their benches [and] passed the day in eating and drinking, and enjoying themselves; and they performed the *tauqui* called *alançitua saqui* [a dance] in red shirts down to their feet . . . . They gave thanks to the Creator for having spared them to see that day, and prayed that they might pass another year without sickness . . . . "

After Inti, the god with the most power was Illapa, who represented rain, thunder, and lightning. Illapa was also the god of war. Pictures of Illapa showed a man's form in the sky holding a war club in one hand and a slingshot in the other. These two weapons were the principal weapons of the Inca military.

Inca subjects worshipped a number of other gods and goddesses, all related to nature. Mama Quilla—the moon—was the honored sister and wife of Inti, the sun god. Shrines to Mama Quilla featured silver

IN THEIR OWN WORDS

Honoring the Natural World

The Inca religion honored many aspects of the natural world. Some were gods, and some were simply forces of nature that were offered respect and admiration. Cronista Garcilaso de la Vega explains the role of thunder, lightning, and rainbows:

Thunder and lightning together were called by the simple word illapa; they . . . were looked up to as attendants of the Sun, and they were believed to live in the air, but not in the sky. They also respected the rainbow, whose beautiful colors they admired, and which the Inca kings used in their coats of arms.

(Source: de la Vega, Garcilaso. *The Incas: The Royal Commentaries of the Inca.* Translated by Maria Jolas from the critical, annotated edition of Alain Gheerbrant. New York: The Orion Press, 1961.)

objects because the people believed that silver came from the "tears of the moon." During a lunar eclipse, the people believed Mama Quilla had been swallowed up by a puma or a snake. To undo this tragedy, the people pounded drums, blew horns and pipes, and made a great noise. Their efforts were rewarded when the moon reappeared.

Priests and priestesses honored Pacha Mama (Mother Earth) and Mama Cocha (Mother Water) by offering sacrifices to them to ensure good harvests.

The Incas honored their gods at a principal shrine in Cuzco called the Coricancha. This building was made of dark stone and was decorated inside with gold and silver. There were buildings set aside to worship the six main gods, including Inti, Illapa, and Mama Quilla. However, many holy places existed throughout the Inca Empire.

The Incas built and maintained spirit dwellings and holy places, called *huacas*, which could be caves, springs, oddly shaped rocks, or specially built shrines. Battlegrounds and cemeteries could also be honored as *huacas*.

The idea of a spiritual place included spiritual objects, such as amulets (an ornament or small piece of jewelry thought to protect against evil, danger, or disease), statues, relics, and both animals and plants designated as holy. Thus, *huaca* came to mean all religious places and objects connected with gods and worship. Damaging or destroying a *huaca* was a crime.

The Incas worshipped the sun, moon, and the dramatic forces of nature, such as thunder and lightening. They believed in an afterlife. For them, the body was possessed by two different souls. When the person died, each soul followed a separate path. One path led to the person's origin. The nature of that origin depended on how virtuous and productive a life the person had led. The other soul remained in the body and would stay there forever once the corpse had been mummified.

Bodies were treated with herbs and wrapped in a mummy bundle of cloth. Then the mummy was buried. To provide for the soul that stayed with the body, the mummy bundle contained many necessary personal items. A goldsmith might be buried with his tools, a woman with her loom and yarn for weaving, a potter with jars from his workshop.

The Sapa Incas were also mummified, but they were not buried. The Sapa Inca was considered to be a god and therefore could not really die. The palace in which a Sapa Inca lived his life became his shrine

The first frozen Inca mummy ever found was discovered by American archaeologist Johan Reinhard in 1995. Remarkably well preserved this mummy of a 12–14 year old girl has been displayed around the world and now rests in Arequipa, Peru.

for the afterlife. There, the mummy lived in splendor amid his former wives, servants, and household guards, who continued to serve his mummified body. During the Festival of the Dead in November, mummified Sapa Incas were carried on golden litters from their palaces to the plaza in Cuzco. They were honored with feasts, music, and dancing, and offered gifts of cloth, gold, and food.

Daily life among the Incas depended heavily on the fate of each person, as seen by diviners. These people foretold the future. They could predict illness, bad luck, and criminal investigations, and also told people what sacrifices should be made to head off these unhappy events. Occasionally, future events were foretold by reading coca leaves. Sacrifices to the gods were the only way to overcome bad luck. These sacrifices included food (primarily potatoes, llamas, or guinea pigs), cloth, or other handcrafts.

Religion was as carefully organized as every other part of Inca life. There was a head priest, the *uma uillca*, who would be roughly equivalent to a pope or archbishop in Christianity. Beneath the head priest were *hatun uillcas*, whose jobs were like those of regional administrators. The *hatun uillcas* supervised the religious communities of the Inca Empire. At the lowest level of priests were the *yana uillcas*, who served as local priests and would compare with parish priests, synagogue rabbis, or church ministers today.

Priests had several different duties, including teaching the local people about the gods and rites performed in the gods' honor. Priests also heard confessions of commoners and gave them a way to be forgiven for their sins. This could be a physical punishment, such as being struck with a rock on the back of the head. The most severe was a form of banishment that required a man or woman to live in the wilderness, find their food in the woods, and keep away from other people. The loneliness of banishment was painful for people who depended on community life for survival.

Women served the Inca religion as chosen women. Regional administrators selected these women—*acllas*—for service by the age of 10. The girls were chosen based on their physical beauty and could not refuse the honor. *Acllas* studied in the Acllahuasi, which housed them, and many became teachers for other *acllas*. They were called *mamacunas*, or guardian mothers.

As young girls, the *acllas* were trained to follow one of three paths: priestess, wife, or sacrifice. A girl might become priestess of the sun or the moon, whose primary job was weaving fine cloth for the Sapa Inca, preparing food and cloth as offerings to Inca gods and goddesses, and participating in rituals. The most beautiful girls often became secondary wives for the Sapa Inca or other nobles, since the nobility could have more than one wife. The final group provided human sacrifices, although such offerings were not common.

At the height of the Inca Empire, there may have been as many as 1,500 *acllas*, whom the Spanish called "the virgins of the sun." When an *aclla* who was destined to become a priestess reached adulthood, she spoke vows that committed her to the religious life. These priestesses rarely saw any men—not even a high priest or the Sapa Inca. If a priestess took a lover, both were executed.

The people paid taxes to support the priests and *acllas*, supplying the religious community with wool for spinning and weaving, food, leather, cloth, gold and silver objects for temples and shrines, and

The Woman of Ancón

The mummy of an Inca woman was found in Ancón, Peru, in 1976. Her mummy was in excellent condition, wrapped in several layers of fine cloth. When archaeologists Karen Stothert and Roger Ravines studied the mummy, they realized the woman had been an excellent weaver, much honored by her friends and family. In her wrappings, Stothert and Ravines found four burial shrouds. The corpse's head had been placed on a pillow, then wrapped. She wore rings on her hands. Within the mummy bundle lay a workbasket filled with weaving materials. There were weaving and spinning tools. She also had household goods wrapped in the bundle. These included corn, dried fruit, beans, silver rings, shells, and valuable coca leaves.

This somewhat fanciful engraving of an Inca priest was done by French artist L. F. Labrousse in 1796 to illustrate a book about exotic lands.

religious objects. Items given to the temples and shrines were used as sacrificial offerings or to maintain the religious community. Stored food provided feasts at public festivals.

Among the many offerings made to the gods were daily sacrifices of animals and occasional human sacrifices. Unlike the Aztecs, the Incas did not believe that regular human sacrifice had any advantage over sacrificing animals or cloth. They did believe that specific gods should receive very specific sacrifices. Viracocha, founder of the world, received the sacrifice of brown llamas, while white llamas were dedicated to Inti, and speckled or spotted animals became gifts to Illapa.

Human sacrifice was made only when sacrificing animals did not seem sufficient, such as during major disasters—earthquakes, drought, famine, or eclipses. The most common victims were girls and boys about 10 years of age, although some victims were infants. Historians believe child sacrifices may have taken place twice a year.

CHAPTER 6

INCA ART, SCIENCE, AND CULTURE

THE INCAS WERE PRACTICAL PEOPLE, AND MOST INCA ART was also practical. The Incas admired production, not original designs. They saw no use for art that showed landscapes or portraits, or that interpreted the human experience.

Critics claim that Inca art shows little imagination because Inca artists used the same themes over and over. However, few weavers today could produce cloth as intricate and tightly woven as the Incas did. Even with modern tools, today's potters would have difficulty reproducing the fine pottery and glazes of the Moche. And few rulers today enjoy gardens decorated with perfect gold replicas of corn, butterflies, and guinea pigs.

Cronista Garcilaso de la Vega described (in *The Incas: Royal Commentaries*) the Sapa Inca's garden: "There were fields of corn with silver stalks and golden ears, on which the leaves, grains, and even the corn silk were shown. In addition, there were all kinds of gold and silver animals in these gardens, such as rabbits, mice, lizards, snakes, butterflies, foxes, and wildcats; there were birds set in the trees, and others bent over the flowers, breathing in their nectar."

WEAVING

Although every woman and many men could make cloth, expert textile weavers were especially valued for their talents. In their hands, yellow, red, brown, and gold yarns came together in detailed geometric patterns. Only nobles wore patterned cloth, and the clothing of lesser nobles never outshone the tunics of the Sapa Inca.

OPPOSITE

Inca-inspired arts remain a part of Peruvian culture. Here, girls dance at Cuzco's Inti Raymi Inca festival celebrating the winter solstice.

Accomplished male weavers and the *mamacunas*, guardian mother teachers of the chosen women, produced woolen cloth made from the fleece of llamas, alpacas, and vicuñas. Cotton yarn,

A Tradition in Textiles

"In the Andes of Peru, weavings are important to every Inca family. Every village has its own weaving patterns. There are thousands of techniques, layouts, styles, and practices associated with Peruvian weaving. We draw on a tradition of more than 2,000 years and we are still weaving today," says Nilda Callañaupa, director of the Center for Traditional Textiles of Cuzco, in "A Message from Nilda Callañaupa" that appears on the center's Web site.

Established in 1996, the Center for Traditional Textiles of Cuzco works to preserve ancient textile skills. The center is a living museum in which wool and thread are spun and woven in both traditional and non-traditional ways.

Weaving has religious and historical connections. The Inca citizens honored Mother Earth (Pacha Mama) in woven cloth. Spinning, dyeing, and weaving is a record of the hard work of the civilization's women, from the lowest peasant wife to the noble *coya*, the primary wife of the Inca ruler.

The center brings weaving skills into modern education by partnering skilled weavers with community children. It rewards outstanding artistry by displaying the works of weavers and offering financial prizes for particularly beautiful work. The center also provides a place for weavers to work their craft and demonstrate their skills for the public.

To record the historical significance of textiles in the Andes Mountains, the center interviewed more than 80 weavers. They documented traditional patterns and identified weavers who produce the same geometric and figure patterns so honored in the days of Pachacuti (r. 1438–1471) and Tupac Yupanqui (r. 1471–1493).

Callañaupa serves as both director and principal weaver for the Center for Traditional Textiles of Cuzco. She spins raw materials (cotton, llama wool, alpaca wool, and vicuña wool—the wool of a wild relative of the llama) into yarn in the same way her ancestors did.

While the center offers works for sale, buyers should expect to pay a high price for such quality weaving. A tapestry made of vicuña wool, for example, might cost as much as $5,000. The price reflects the scarcity of vicuña, the difficulty in collecting enough of the wool to produce cloth, and the time invested by the weaver.

either alone or blended with wool, was also common, particularly in coastal regions where wool clothing was too hot to wear. Weavers created woven, repeating patterns of rectangles, squares, and diamonds, or embroidered animals, such as pumas, llamas, and birds, onto finished cloth.

GOLD AND SILVER

The Inca culture described gold as "sweat of the sun," and gold decorated the palaces of the Sapa Incas and the Inca nobility, and the Coricancha—the temple of the sun. Despite having only very basic tools, goldsmiths and silversmiths made remarkably fine work. Earplugs made of fine strands of metal, mother-of-pearl mosaics against a gold background, gem-encrusted knives and plates, and funeral masks were owned by the emperor and crown princes.

In fact, the emperor's household fairly glowed with bright golden plates, wall plaques, utensils, jugs, and *aryballos* (bottles). The Incas did not use much furniture, but the Sapa Inca did sit on a golden stool or ride in a gold and gem-encrusted litter. (He was shielded from the sun by umbrellas made of tropical bird feathers.)

Inca goldsmiths and silversmiths produced jewelry and artifacts as delicate as any produced in Europe at the time—yet without the special tools designed for such work. Goldsmiths pounded bright metal into thin sheets using only stones. They laid the gold on a large flat rock, then hammered with smaller, rounded stones in their hands. The gold was heated, pounded, and cooled again, repeating the process until the gold sheet was paper-thin. Smiths also created alloys of gold and silver or other precious metals and annealed (strengthened) the metal by heating it in special furnaces.

The Inca furnace was a technological marvel. Made of clay, Inca furnaces reached temperatures up to about 1,830 degrees Fahrenheit. To reach such high temperatures, furnaces required steady blasts of air blown onto the coals. For this the Incas used long copper pipes and human labor. About a dozen pipes were inserted into blast holes in the furnace base, and workers blew into the pipes and forced more air over the coals.

Using sharp, pointed tools, goldsmiths embossed the gold (created a design on the surface) with images of the sun, pumas, birds, or feathers. Goldsmiths, like most other artists, lived in city of Cuzco and were

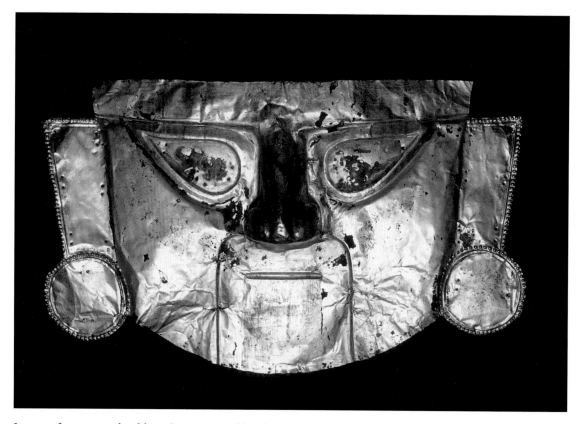

Inca craftsmen used gold extensively. This Chimu mask is an example of their workmanship and creativity.

supported by the government. They lived in houses, ate food, and wore clothing provided by the Sapa Inca's administrators.

So fine was Inca gold and silver work that Spanish conquistadors and historians remarked on its quality. In 1613, Spaniard Juan de Torquemada stated that Inca smiths produced jewelry "greatly surpassing that of our Spanish jewelers because they could make birds whose heads, tongues, and wings could be made to move, and animals in whose paws they place trinkets that seemed to dance" (as quoted in *Incas: Lords of Gold and Glory*).

Archaeologists have discovered many gold and silver artifacts in Inca burial mounds. They have uncovered silver statues of musicians playing little flutes, hammered gold goblets and pitchers, and shiny pectorals (chest ornaments) cut from thin sheets of gold. Personal items, such as tweezers for removing whiskers and knives for cutting meat, lay among the bones of Incas long dead. These buried artifacts accompanied only nobles into the afterlife—commoners never owned precious metal items.

POTTERY

Like weaving, pottery and ceramic skills developed many centuries before the Inca Empire rose to power. Examples of Chavín (900–200 B.C.E.) and Moché (100–700) pottery have been uncovered in ruins, temples, and burial sites. These pieces include vessels used for drinking beer, large urns and jars to store or cook foods, round vases, and small statues. The ceramics of these cultures have complex geometric patterns, birds and animals, occasionally human forms, and human figures in action.

Although Inca pottery was decorated, the ideal piece was useful and easy to produce in large numbers. The decorations and shapes of ceramic pieces were borrowed from earlier cultures. These somewhat plain clay jugs and crockery were never designed for palace use. Only gold and silver were satisfactory for a ruler who claimed he was the son of the sun.

FUN AND GAMES

For all their beauty, gold jewelry, textiles, and pottery resulted from hard work, which was the guiding force of Inca life. Work, not play, dominated the Inca daily schedule. There was little time for fun and games.

Athletic contests were only open to sons of the nobility and were associated with male puberty rites. Foot races at full speed down an Andes mountainside often provided many more wounded than winners, but they were one source of public entertainment. Young men also played war games in which they demonstrated their skills with slingshots, clubs, lances, or bolas.

Hunting provided sport with a positive result: meat. It was against the law to hunt in the Sapa Inca's forests, and anyone who did was executed when caught. A government-authorized hunt provided guanacos, vicuñas (both wild relatives of the llama), deer, and other meats for festivals and for drying and storing. Hunters used slingshots and lances—weapons common to the battlefield—to hunt large game. Communities delighted in the hunt because it brought a change in work patterns, as well as dancing, feasting, music, and plenty of drinking.

When nobles got together, they often played a gambling game called *aylloscas* for high stakes. The rules for playing *aylloscas* have been lost over time. However, *cronistas* recount stories in which winners acquired new lands, homes, or even young wives from the losers.

Children played with tops, balls, and a type of dice made from bits of pottery. Girls may have had simple dolls, although it is likely that care of younger siblings replaced playing house. Children, like their parents, had little playtime and many responsibilities, including helping in the fields, harvesting crops, preparing food, and keeping their homes clean. Among the more pleasant tasks for children might have been searching in forests and meadows for medicinal herbs.

MUSIC

Musicians were among the many artisans who lived and worked under Inca rule. Panpipes (a musical instrument made from a row of short pipes tied together), called *sikuris* or *zampoña*, have been part of Andes music for centuries, and the haunting notes of the panpipes sang across the mountains and valleys of the Inca Empire. In Inca times, pipers made their own instruments from bamboo. Thin reeds (*chillis* or *icas*) produced high soprano notes, while flat, thick reeds (*toyos*) made the bass and baritone notes.

The pipers formed a circle around their conductor, alternating notes between two or more pipers. They played the pipes by blowing across the opening at the top of each reed. Making music with panpipes is much like blowing across glass bottles. Air moving across the hollow space creates a tone. The larger the pipes, the lower the notes and the stronger the breath required to make a sound. Thus, *toyos* players needed powerful lungs.

Flutes, rattles, and drums accompanied the panpipes. Musi-

CONNECTIONS

Inca Music Today

Traditional music is still used to mark life events in the Andes. A house blessing or the birth of a child is a common reason for a celebration. Andes people have maintained many Inca religious customs, such as planting and harvest festivals, during which music fills the thin mountain air. Community events draw pipers, drummers, and flute players to town plazas, recreating the rhythms of their Inca past.

Several modern music groups play traditional Inca or Andes music. One of the most dramatic groups is Andes Manta. Four brothers of the Lopez family make up the quartet that plays traditional Andes folk music on more than 35 authentic Inca instruments, including the panpipes, *quenas* (flutes), various rattles, and drums. Andes Manta performs in Spanish and in Quechua, the language of the Incas, providing a lingering memory of ancient times long gone. Their music can be heard on their Web site.

cians made flutes (*quenas*) from bamboo and the leg bones of animals. *Quenas* range from small instruments for high notes to large ones for low notes. Their sound resembles that of a recorder. Another flute, a wooden *tarka*, provided music for religious rites and had a tone similar to an oboe.

Rattles added rhythm to Inca music. The *chác-chás* consists of a number of llama or goat hooves on a string that produce clicking noises when shaken. The *chaucha* is a natural rattle made from a dried seedpod with many small beans inside. This instrument produces a noise like Mexican maracas, and has been part of traditional Andes music since long before the Spanish arrived in Peru. Small rattles were attached to the ankles or wrists of dancers, enabling them to produce their own rhythms as they moved.

Another interesting rattle is the *palo de lluvia*, which means "rain stick." To make a traditional rain stick, a musician drills holes in a long bamboo reed and slides thin sticks through the holes. Dried beans or pebbles partially fill the bamboo tube, and the ends are sealed. To play the instrument, the musician turns it upside down. The beans rattle against the sticks as they roll and produce a sound like rainfall. Like the panpipes and flutes, rattles are still used in traditional Andes music.

Drums have been around since humans first struck hollow logs with animal bones. The Andes version of the drum was made by stretching animal skins over hollow sections of wood. Military drums followed a dark tradition: The drum skins came from the bodies of slain enemies. The pounding sound of sticks, bones, or hands against a human-skin drum struck terror into the Incas' enemies.

The Incas did not make metal horns, such as trumpets or bugles. However, they did use conch-shell trumpets for military, religious, and civil ceremonies. The military signaled the start of battle by blowing the conch. The bellow of a conch also called the faithful to temples and plazas for religious rituals. And in civil life, *chasquis* (postal runners) blew on the conch to alert the next post of their arrival.

DANCE

Like music, dance expresses the emotions of the people. For the Inca people, dancing provided a release from work and a way to worship their gods and actively participate in rituals. Traditional Inca dances told stories in the same way that some ballets do today. It also allowed

Peruvians carry on the music and dance traditions of their Inca ancestors.

unmarried men to pursue a potential bride, commemorate a life event such as a new child or a death, and have some fun.

Today, more than 700 dances exist from pre-Inca and empire times. These dances usually involve many dancers, some for men alone, others just for women, and still others for couples. One popular dance form, called *harawi*, originated with Inca poetry, and is really a long, sad song about lost or unfulfilled love and loneliness. The *huayno*, performed at major festivals, features couples dancing to a pounding rhythm, moving together yet rarely touching.

Today's popular folk dances in the Andes blend the traditional dances of Inca times with modern rhythms. Dance continues to be an important part of festivals and celebrations. The instruments and dance steps of Inca days blend with electric guitars and African rhythms to create the new music of the Andes.

LEGENDS AND DRAMA

While Inca music and dance have been preserved, the culture's literary heritage has nearly disappeared. Without a written language, plays, legends, and poems were passed down by oral tradition.

Amautas (wise men) devised clever comedies and tragedies that were performed for the Sapa Inca and his court. Cronista Garcilaso de la Vega wrote (in *The Incas: Royal Commentaries*), "The actors were . . . Incas or nobles, *curacas*, captains, and even camp commanders: each one, in fact, being obliged to possess in real life the quality, or occupy the function, of the role he interpreted. The themes of the tragedies were always taken from history, and usually related the triumphs and valorous acts of one of the early kings, or some other hero of the empire."

Sadly, the great majority of these historical dramas vanished once the Spanish Catholic priests became powerful in Peru. The priests decided this kind of entertainment was heathen, because many plays mentioned Inca gods or referred to Sapa Incas as gods. Therefore, they would not allow myths or plays with Inca religious symbols or topics to be performed in public. Longer plays and myths were lost because they were never performed and could not be remembered. The few remaining bits of Inca literature are poetry and short legends—material that was easy to recite in homes.

Even the greatest chroniclers of Inca history found only a few samples of Inca literature. Garcilaso de la Vega recorded several short poems, translating them into Spanish for his reading audience.

MEDICINE

Inca medicine was based on the use of healing herbs. These herbs were collected by women and children. Herbal healing

---

IN THEIR OWN WORDS

The Rainbow

In *Black Rainbow*, author John Bierhorst presents myths and legends of the Andes Mountains that have survived to this day. This excerpt explains the creation of a rainbow, a powerful symbol in Inca times and a common source of interest to today's Andean people.

When the sun comes up and a mist is in the air and the whole sky is brilliant, then from a natural fountain the rainbow is born, stretching forth in an enormous arc.

But it fears the people on earth; their faces are much too lively, and it draws itself back through the sky like a braided rope of many colors.

There were once some little boys who set out to find its feet. But its toes are made of crystal and it always hides them. So the little boys were unable to find what they were looking for and they threw stones at the rainbow.

When the rainbow enters the body of a man or woman, then the person becomes gravely ill. But the sick person will be cured if he unravels a ball of yarn made of seven colors.

(Source: Bierhorst, John. *Black Rainbow*. New York: Farrar, Strauss and Giroux, 1976.)

Felipe Guaman Poma de Ayala made this drawing of Incas working with herbs and plants, which they used to make medicines.

during Inca times was very much like it is today. Few Andes villages have doctors or access to regular medical care, so understanding the healing properties of natural herbs is vital for good health.

In Inca times, medical care consisted of elderly women who knew how to use herbs and doctors who knew how to stop bleeding, amputate limbs on battlefields, and heal illness. A group of wandering healers, called *collahuayas*, who came from Lake Titicaca, were so skilled that they treated the royal family.

Inca medicine developed separately from European and Far Eastern medicine, yet Inca healers used two medical procedures that were common in Europe and Asia: bloodletting and trepanning. Bloodletting means removing blood in a controlled way. It was believed to cure some diseases. The Inca took blood from the part of the body that was nearest the point of the patient's suffering. So, for example, when a patient had a headache, they bled the patient's forehead.

Trepanning—cutting holes into the skull for medical purposes— was common on the battlefields, where men struck by clubs often had crushed skulls. Often, coca and other drugs were used to numb the patient before surgery began. Relieving pressure on the brain from such wounds or removing bone splinters were not the only reasons for trepanning. Mental illnesses and physical problems such as epilepsy and migraine headaches may have been other reasons for brain surgery.

It appears that peoples of the Andes performed brain surgery on living patients earlier in history and more often than anywhere else in the world. Archaeologists have dated trepanned skulls back to roughly 400 B.C.E. Literally hundreds of skulls with a variety of circular or rectangular holes cut into them have been found in burial mounds throughout Peru. This is many more than exists from other civilizations that performed trepanning.

Scientists discovered that, in some cultures, trepanning was performed on corpses as a way to release the spirit or soul of the deceased. Inca incisions, on the other hand, were performed on living bone. Examination of Inca trepanned skulls reveals that bone healed, and a surprising number of the patients lived.

Healing involved the entire community. Women assumed responsibility for care and feeding of the sick, and this included anyone within the *ayllu*. Since people rarely lived alone, someone was always on hand to tend to a wounded or sick person. Traveling healers consulted with local herbal experts in choosing the best prescription for any illness.

The Inca culture left nothing to chance, however, and also used supernatural forces to aid the healing process. Ritual sacrifice, such as burning coca leaves or cloth, encouraged the interest of the appropriate gods.

Although people of the Andes cultures did not experience widespread diseases such as smallpox, measles, or flu before the arrival of the Spanish, they did get serious illnesses. Evidence indicates that tuberculosis, malaria, syphilis, and leprosy existed in the Andes during Inca times. So did intestinal and stomach worms, such as tapeworms and pinworms, and lice infestations.

The lack of a written language held back the advance of Inca medicine. Knowledge of how to diagnose and treat disease had to be handed from parent to child, and many prescriptions were

CONNECTIONS

Herbal Remedies

Herbal remedies in Inca times reduced fevers and coughs, healed broken bones, and stopped itching from insect or animal bites. The same herbs perform the same functions in today's Andes Mountains. Many of the ingredients used in these medicines are the same as those used in today's prescription drugs, as well, including quinine and coca.

Matecclu, a wetland plant with a single leaf on a narrow stem, provides effective treatment for eye infections. Corn, one of the staples of the Inca diet, helps prevent the formation of kidney and bladder stones. Applications of a concoction made from *chilca* leaves relieves achy joints, while sarsaparilla, a soft drink ingredient, relieves painful sores.

Of course, coca, which held a primary place in the Inca pharmacy, is still used to treat altitude sickness and relieve hunger and fatigue. The *molle* tree provides berries for making beer, bark to improve the healing of open wounds, and twigs that make excellent toothbrushes.

Herbalists in modern Peru sell their remedies at open markets. Along with the package of herbs, patients can get a quick diagnosis and instructions on how to use the herbs.

probably lost. Luckily, Spanish priests recorded local remedies in their journals, preserving many recipes for herbal tonics, infusions, and ointments.

MATHEMATICS AND SCIENCE

As with medicine, Inca science and mathematics did not advance much during the years of the empire because there was no written language. Discoveries were often lost because people with scientific interest could not write down the experiments they did or what they learned from those experiments. This also prevented them from sharing these discoveries more widely with others.

Geologic events (earthquakes and volcanic eruptions) and severe weather patterns (droughts or blizzards) were, to the Inca mind, the result of angry gods. The people attempted to soothe the gods' anger by sacrificing food, cloth, and, occasionally, humans.

Astronomy, a subject that captivated Mayan and Egyptian minds, generated limited interest among the Inca. People observed the movements of the sun, the moon, and the planet Venus. They also recognized the shift in the sun's path that accompanied the winter solstice, when the sun reaches its lowest point in the sky, and the summer solstice, when the sun reaches its highest point in the sky. In Cuzco, Inca architects built eight towers, four facing the rising sun and four facing the setting sun.

IN THEIR OWN WORDS

Waking the Moon

Eclipses caused great terror in the Inca Empire. Cronista Garcilaso de la Vega described the attitude of the Incas toward solar and lunar eclipses in his book, *The Incas: Royal Commentaries*:

For them, when the Sun was in an eclipse, some misdemeanor committed in the kingdom had irritated it, since, at that moment, its countenance [face] had the disturbed look of a man in anger, and they predicted, as astrologists do, the imminence of some severe chastisement [punishment]. During an eclipse of the Moon . . . they said it was ill, and that if it continued in this state, it would die and fall down to earth; that it would crush them all under the weight of its body, and that this event would be the end of the world. At this thought, they were seized with such fright that they began to play on horns and trumpets, timpani and drums . . . they would tie up their dogs both large and small, and beat them hard to make them bark and bay at the Moon . . . they thought, if the Moon heard them baying for her, she would awaken from the dream in which illness held her a prisoner.

(Source: de la Vega, Garcilaso. *The Incas: The Royal Commentaries of the Inca, Garcilaso de la Vega*. Translated by Maria Jolas from the critical, annotated edition of Alain Gheerbrant. New York: The Orion Press, 1961.)

The towers were set so that the sun's path could be traced and noted. On the solstices, the sun left no shadow beside key columns.

The study of plants and animals also held little interest, except as they helped to increase crops or raise healthy llama herds. Through experimentation, the Incas developed new varieties of potatoes and corn that produced more or larger vegetables, greater resistance to frost or cold, or increased production in arid regions.

Mathematics in the Inca world related to practical applications that were developed through experience. Again, the Incas had no written numerical system, so more advanced mathematics never developed. However, mathematical calculations enabled the Incas to survey and portion out acreage among the *ayllus*. *Quipus*, the Inca knot database, recorded crop and manufacturing yields, assessed taxes, and recorded payments. In addition to the *quipu*, the Incas developed a counting board, *the yupana*, that used dots and circles to keep track of numbers.

The Incas relied heavily on their version of the decimal system. Groups of 10 were important to the government and within the military. The basic unit of civil management was the *ayllu*, a group of 10 households. Similarly, the basic unit in the military was a troop of 10 soldiers. From there, Inca management developed larger elements with a leader for each level. A *curaca* never managed a group of 1,046 households, since such uneven amounts were unacceptable. Instead, the "extra" 46 households were folded into a new precinct, realigning perhaps dozens of communities to establish precise units.

When the Spanish arrived in the Inca Empire, they were astounded by the accuracy of the Inca census. The government authorities knew how many people lived in the empire, as well as their age, sex, marital status, profession, social class, productivity, and location. With advanced technology and supercomputers available to the United States government today, a national census is taken every 10 years and the resulting statistics allow for various error rates. The Incas took their census, reassigned agricultural plots, and assessed taxes every year, with no errors.

BUILDING AND ARCHITECTURE

Inca architects and engineers had the greatest understanding of and use for practical mathematics. They produced accurate models of buildings,

Earthquake-Proof Masonry

In light of the damage done by earthquakes in recent years, architects might well consider using Inca techniques to join stone to stone. The basic materials of Inca stonework were simple: locally available limestone or granite, simple stone tools, water, and sand.

An Inca architect developed a plan for a building, complete with a model. Skilled masons (stone workers) and builders marked out the foundation according to the model. Then came the clever work—fitting stone to stone.

Stones were cut at a quarry and moved to the building site by brute force, because the Incas did not have wheels or pulleys to lessen the burden of moving stones weighing many tons. While it is impossible to know for sure, some scientists believe the Incas used levers to hoist the building stones onto smaller rounded stones, making them easier to move.

At the construction site, the huge stone blocks were sorted by size and shape, fitting the pieces together much like a jigsaw puzzle. At that point, a skilled mason shaped two stones to fit side by side. He did this by carving some areas that curved in and some that curved out.

Says author John Hemming in *Monuments of the Incas*, "There was no secret formula, no magic chemical that could shape the stones, nothing but cutting with stone axes, abrasion with sand and water, and the skill and dedication of Inca masons." These are primitive techniques, but the fit between stones was so tight that many of these walls remain standing today. The funeral buildings at Wilcawain in northern Peru were built nearly 1,000 years ago. In a region plagued by earthquakes, they have outlasted Spanish architecture and modern construction projects.

towns, and local geographic features. They understood elevations (how the land rises), angles, and how the shape of the land affects building plans. Of all the legacies left by the Incas, surely their architectural achievements are the most enduring.

The Inca army marched along paved roads that stretched from the empire's extreme north to its southern border. The roads, mostly paved with stone, connected region to region, city to city, with all roads eventually leading to Cuzco.

The roads followed two basic systems. The Andes system was built along the mountain passes and valleys. The coastal system ran along the Pacific Ocean. Each area presented obstacles. The mountains were steep, dangerous, and rugged, while the coastal roads passed through dry desert with its blowing sands.

East-west roads connected the north-south highways and made travel to any region easy. At its greatest, the empire maintained more than 15,625 miles of roads.

The roads were the main transportation routes for government officials, battalions of soldiers, and shipments of food and goods (mostly tax payments). Every few miles along the roads, rest areas provided shelter, food, and clothing for travelers. These rest areas were supported by the Sapa Inca and maintained by government workers. Transportation hubs, called *tampu*, existed at key crossroads and were equipped with huge lodges for housing dozens of travelers or the military. Huts along the roads housed *chasquis*, the Inca equivalent of a postal service.

Mountainous areas have fast-flowing rivers and deep ravines that seem impossible to cross. But Inca engineers devised several styles of bridges. Engineers preferred to use tree trunks as bridges over narrow streams or crevices. They built stone bridges by laying slabs across wider gaps.

Bridges made of leather, hemp rope, and agave fiber were called "braided bridges," and were remarkably strong and durable. A bridge of this sort spans the Apurimac River near the present-day town of Qheswachaka.

However, true Inca ingenuity came with the *huaros, uruyas,* and *tarabitas,* which resembled modern-day cable cars. Thick willow branches were interwoven to create baskets or gondolas, which were suspended from ropes made of strong *chawar* fiber. The ropes, fastened to tree trunks or boulders, were strong enough to support one or two people in each gondola. When the Spanish arrived, they transported their horses across ravines using harnesses hooked over these ropes. Says historian Carmen Bernand in *The Incas: People of the Sun,* "Whereas in the valleys river crossings were made by raft, the mountain torrents were crossed using rope bridges or baskets suspended from cables. Moreover, all these crossing points were supervised, and nobody could carry a load across without paying a toll."

Extensive building programs required millions of hours of labor, which were provided mainly through the *mit'a*. Every *puric* contributed a few weeks each year to the government, during which he was assigned to whatever project was the local priority. *Mit'a* projects built and maintained roads, bridges, government buildings, irrigation ditches

This is the last Inca-built straw bridge in Peru. It spans the Apurimac River near Cuzco.

and canals, and temples. Hundreds of skilled masons, architects, and engineers kept busy throughout the year, contributing the knowledge needed to oversee every project.

Of great interest to today's architects was the Inca use of geometric shapes in building. Trapezoids (four-sided figures in which only two sides are parallel) were used as doorways, windows, alcoves, and niches. The wider end of the trapezoid served as part of the foundation, and the narrow end supported the walls above, much as a lintel supports a doorway.

The northeast wall of Inca Roca's palace, built in the 14th century, is an excellent example of the Inca use of geometric blocks. Some blocks in this palace are 12-sided, yet each stone links perfectly with its neighbors. The blocks were carved at the site from local material. Most doors and windows were made of multiple blocks.

The Inca civilization emphasized function and practicality over beauty—except for the use of water. Architects and engineers showed a surprising preference for the artistic when incorporating springs and streams into their work. Wherever possible, the flow of water was altered so that natural springs bubbled up into decorative pools or streams gushed from stone spouts. In palaces, water spilled out of stone pipes into large pools, then fell into smaller basins and flowed out along open aqueducts.

While many examples of Inca architecture remain, historians believe that more would have survived if the Spanish had not been so determined to

Recreating an Inca Rope Bridge

The Spanish were amazed to find sturdy bridges made of nothing but fiber rope spanning the deep Andes ravines. In 2007, students from Massachusetts Institute of Technology (MIT) in Cambridge, Massachusetts, decided to learn about this Inca technology by building a rope bridge of their own.

The students made a fiber rope bridge 60 feet long and two feet wide across a dry basin between two campus buildings. The ropes were made following directions read in the chronicles of Cronista Garcilaso de la Vega. The students wove together 12 strands of twine to make each primary rope. Then three of these 12-ply ropes were braided to make the major cables.

Fourteen students met two evenings a week and occasional afternoons to braid the ropes. They estimated that they spent a total of 360 hours twisting rope and used 50 miles of sisal twine. When the students walked across the bridge, it proved to be strong and safe.

Machu Picchu

The mountaintop retreat of Machu Picchu (in Quechua the name means "old peak") remained hidden in the Andes for centuries, until Hiram Bingham, a Yale University professor, found the site in 1911. In truth, the ruins were never "lost," since local people always knew exactly where Machu Picchu was—at the top of a 9,000-foot mountain.

The site contains a remarkable city that was once a country palace for the Sapa Inca. Hidden by mountain mists are more than 150 houses, temples, baths, storage rooms, and palaces. The site has a cemetery, facilities for processing grain, and a plaza for festivals. One of the most remarkably beautiful features of Machu Picchu is the many fountains, which were created from natural springs that ripple down rock walls or pool in sunken tubs.

The stonework shows off the skills of Inca masons. Walls are built of cut stones that are fitted so tightly that a knife will not pass between them. Some of the individual building stones weigh more than 50 tons.

Artifacts found at Machu Picchu include cups and urns of bronze, copper, and silver, ceramic plates and bowls, bracelets, pins, earrings, and tools such as knives and axes. There was no gold.

There were no royal burials at the site, although scientists have found the skeletons of about 174 individuals at Machu Picchu.

The local people were careful never to reveal the location of Machu Picchu to the Spanish. The Spanish conquistadors looted temples and sacred *huacas*, or shrines, while Catholic priests destroyed any religious items they found.

Today, Machu Picchu is a United Nations World Heritage site and a major tourist attraction for people who are willing to hike along the top of the Andes Mountains. Thousands of people have flocked to see the ancient city in the clouds. Unfortunately, their arrival has set off a major disagreement. Conservationists and cultural preservation organizations want to control the tourist traffic, now reaching at least 400,000 people a year, because traffic and trash are damaging the historic site. The stone trail that leads up the Machu Picchu is littered with water bottles, tea bags, and snack wrappers. Regulations to control the waste problem have been ignored by many visitors.

In an effort to reduce the number of visitors, Peru has imposed restrictions that limit the number of people allowed on the trail each day. Only 500 people may visit each day, and they must be accompanied by a registered guide. The must also pay a fee of $50.

erase all elements of non-Christian religion. Unquestionably, the best construction went into building temples, which the Spanish either took apart or built over. The walls of the Coricancha in Cuzco, for example, became the foundation stones for the Spanish-built Church of Santo Domingo, and the Catholic church in Huaitará rises atop a marvelous Inca temple adorned with trapezoidal windows and doorways.

EPILOGUE

IN A SMALL TOWN IN THE ANDES, A MOTHER RISES BEFORE dawn. She blows on the glowing coals in the fireplace to get a fire going. She picks up a bucket and goes to a nearby stream for fresh water. Returning to her one-room adobe hut, she prepares a breakfast of hot corn meal and potatoes.

Her husband and two oldest sons rise and clear away the hand-woven blankets they sleep on. After eating, they join several men and head toward one of the community potato fields. It is an hour's walk from the village. The men carry hoes, shovels, and empty sacks. It is time to harvest potatoes, a backbreaking job that will last for days.

At home, the mother wakes her three youngest children. They eat breakfast as she prepares a lunch of potato soup and *chicha*. Her daughters help her feed the chickens and guinea pigs, milk their one cow, and clean the house. Cleaning takes very little time, since the family owns no furniture other than a plain wooden stool. Dawn breaks as the mother heads to the fields with *almuerzo*, the hot lunch for her family working in the fields.

During the afternoon, the mother prepares dinner for the farm workers and families, who will eat together. She slaughters, skins, and roasts guinea pigs. Her daughters prepare another dish featuring potatoes and two dozen ears of corn. Of course, the workers will drink *chicha*. She wraps the dinner in a blanket and carries the food and beer to the fields on her back. She is joined by other mothers bringing food. They spread out the feast and everyone shares the meal.

The family returns to their home to sleep before beginning yet another day digging potatoes from the hard Andes Mountain soil.

OPPOSITE
Amid a changing modern world, life for Peru's rural people changes little. Here, a man on Amantani Island in Lake Titicaca carries handmade bricks on his back.

This kind of farming remains the economic model for *campesinos*, the people who scrape by in the mountains of Peru and Ecuador today. The family life differs only slightly from peasant life in Inca days. The food, home, and method of making a living are the same.

The clothes are slightly different, although most people still wear material they or their neighbors make themselves. Many remote towns have no electricity or running water. Some have no schools for the children to attend, and most children work to help their families survive.

The spirit of the *ayllu* continues in today's Andes communities. Neighbors and family members plow, plant, and harvest together. They share the crops and work together to prepare and store food, and build or repair homes. As in Inca times, citizens maintain the local roads and irrigation canals, and every family must provide this service or pay a heavy fine.

The community or several neighboring villages support regular local open markets. At these markets, cloth, hats, leather goods, herbs, extra vegetables, and cooked foods such as roasted corn on the cob and grilled llama meat, are sold. Buyers bargain over prices, paying in either currency or by trading their own goods. The markets provide an opportunity for people to exchange goods and gossip.

The main difference between ancient and modern times is the radio. At night, as it gets dark, the family lies on their blankets and listens as Peru's national soccer team takes on Brazil.

THROWING OFF SPANISH RULE

The Inca Empire was once huge, stretching across the borders of today's Peru, Ecuador, Chile, Colombia, and Bolivia. Peru and Ecuador have the strongest links to the ancient empire, while only small portions of the other three countries came under Inca control. Since the Inca Empire disappeared, the five countries have shared several common problems: unstable governments, wars, poverty, threats to natural resources, and human rights struggles for the Native peoples.

From the 16th century to the 19th centuries, Spain ruled former Inca lands with total disregard for the welfare of Native peoples. In the 1800s, national pride gripped the people, and the citizens of the former Inca Empire began a struggle for independence.

Peru declared its independence in 1821. Their revolution was finally successful in 1826, under the leadership of Simón Bolívar (1783–1830).

Bolivia (named after Bolívar) threw out the Spanish in 1824, after a rebel victory led by General Antonio José de Sucre. The new Bolivian government struggled under the leadership of corrupt politicians. In 1836, Bolivia allied itself with Peru, forming a two-country confederation. A little more than 40 years later, this union was dissolved after the War of the Pacific (1879–1884), which forced Peru to give up some land to Chile.

Similar revolutions freed Colombia from Spanish rule in 1819 and Ecuador in 1822. Ecuador, Colombia, and Venezuela formed the Federación de Gran Colombia. Bolívar helped establish the federation. Venezuela and Ecuador left the union in 1830 to form independent countries. In 1885, Colombia formed a republic (a government with elected officials), but political differences among the leaders led to the first of several civil wars. The first civil war (1899–1902) resulted in the deaths of nearly 100,000 citizens. The second (1949–1957) left behind a devastated country after even more deaths.

Chile's independence came as Spain fell to an army led by José de San Martín (1778–1850) in 1817. The country's new leader, Bernardo O'Higgins (1778–1842), established a government that slowly replaced dictatorship with democracy over many years. The third party in the War of the Pacific, Chile, acquired copper-rich territory from Peru and Bolivia at the end of the war.

THE TWENTIETH CENTURY

The 20th century brought more chaos to former Inca territory. In Peru, a string of dictators took over the government. Between 1968 and 1980, Peru came under control of the military. While it was not democratically elected, the military government did carry out extensive land reform. This reform broke up some large land holdings and helped smaller farmers gain land.

Radical groups arose, such as Shining Path (Sendero Luminoso) and the Tupac Amaru Revolutionary Movement. They waged warfare against the military government. When representative government was restored, these groups targeted democratically elected governments. They led brutal attacks that have had far-reaching negative consequences for the civilian population, especially in rural areas. In 2006, former leader Alan Garcia won the presidential election. During Garcia's earlier time in office in the late 1980s, Peru's economy fell

Crowds protest the authoritarian rule of Peruvian president Alberto Fujimori, who served from 1990 to 2000. In 2009 he was found guilty of abuse of authority while in office and was sentenced to prison.

disastrously. Only time will tell whether Garcia will prove successful in the coming years or sink Peru's economy again.

Modern Bolivian politics consists of a series of wars and military takeovers. The country fought a war with Paraguay in the 1930s that caused Bolivia to lose territory. A radical political group made up of miners, the National Revolutionary Movement, seized power in 1943 and again in 1952. While attempts to reform mining and land use failed, the Bolivian people demanded change.

In 1964, guerrilla leader Ernesto "Che" Guevara (1928–1967) led a revolution to overthrow the government. Guevara was a communist who fostered a people's revolution in Bolivia. Communism is a system in which the government controls almost all political and economic activity. It did not produce positive results in Bolivia, and Guevara was killed in a Bolivian jungle in 1967. Guevara's government was followed by a series of oppressive military dictatorships.

Today, Bolivia has a democratically elected president. The current president, Evo Morales, shocked the world economy in 2006 when he put the country's energy industry under government control. This action forced foreign energy companies to sell just over half their holdings to the government or leave Bolivia.

Ecuador's politics over the past century mirrored the military takeovers and dictatorships of its neighbors. Radical student groups rioted in the streets in 1987, the economy failed, new military dictators replaced the old ones—and nothing changed. Continued political unrest, particularly among Native peoples, forced the removal of president Jamil Mahaud in 2000. The country has had three presidents since 1997. President Rafael Correa, elected in 2007, has begun making reforms that will, hopefully, help the country's many poor people.

Colombia's government has been undermined by powerful drug lords who dominate the country, its military, and its police. During the 1980s, political murders became daily events as drug gangs funded highly paid assassins and groups of rebels fighting small military actions.

In the 1990s, radical military groups, such as the Revolutionary Armed Forces of Colombia (FARC) and the National Liberation Army (ELN), terrorized the country, blew up oil pipelines, and kidnapped wealthy businessmen and political figures. In 2002, peace talks with FARC fell apart. President Alvaro Uribe is caught in a difficult position. He has cracked down on FARC and ELN, and is constantly battling against drug traffic out of his country.

Chile's population did no better with their political leaders. President Salvador Allende (1908–1973) elected in the 1970s, tried to establish land reform and have the government run key industries—a type of system called socialism. A military takeover, backed by the United States, threw out Allende. General Augusto Pinochet (b. 1915) took control.

Unemployment rose under Pinochet, as did union strikes and human rights abuses. Government police arrested and killed many opposition leaders. Chilean voters insisted on a presidential election in 1989. Pinochet agreed and lost the election. He remained at the head of Chile's army until 1998.

Chile's current president, Michelle Bachelet, is the fourth consecutive leader from the ruling party. The economy depends on copper, and with the increase in copper prices worldwide, Chile's economy is thriving.

THE EMPIRE TODAY

Traces of Inca greatness and Spanish heritage mingle throughout the five nations that once formed the Inca Empire. Nearly half (45 percent) of Peru's population consists of Quechua people, called *indígenas. Mestizos* (people of mixed Quechua and European heritage) make up another 37 percent. Spanish and Quechua are official Peruvian languages, and many *indígenas* speak only Quechua, the Inca tongue.

Most of the people who today live in the territory of the former Inca Empire follow the Roman Catholic faith. Spanish missions and churches successfully converted the society, and nearly 90 percent of the population belongs to a local parish. However, the dominance of Catholicism does not mean that the ancient gods and religious

Tourism and the Inca Heritage

Archaeological digs and world heritage sites in the Inca region provide the people with a profitable business: tourism. Machu Picchu, Tihuanaco, Chavín Huantar, and Chan Chan draw history lovers who are interested in learning about the Inca culture. UNESCO lists these places as World Heritage Sites, and they are preserved by local and federal agencies. Hiking the Inca Trail, the remains of the ancient Inca mountain road, draws thousands of visitors every year.

traditions have been completely forgotten. For example, Inti Raymi, the celebration honoring the sun god Inti, has been revived in some Andes communities.

The countries that span the Andes Mountains today were all once under the influence of the Inca Empire.

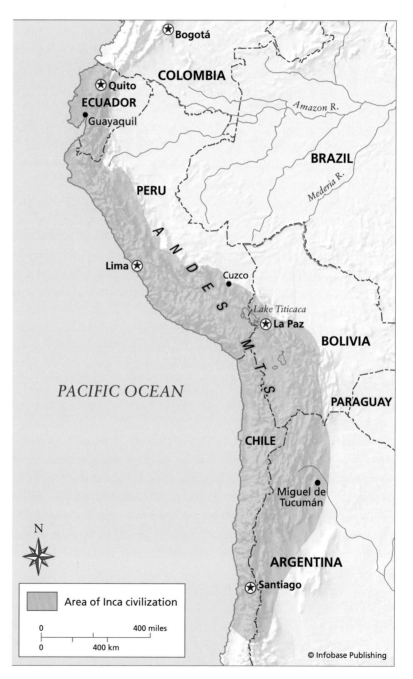

Raising the Dead

In 2002, archaeologists used bulldozers to dig up thousands of Inca mummies buried under a ghetto on the outskirts of Lima, Peru. The bodies were roughly 500 years old, and included at least 2,000 men, women and children. Scientists estimate that the graveyard may contain more than 10,000 dead.

Mummy bundles—groups buried together—held up to seven corpses, binding children and parents together for eternity. According to an article in *National Geographic* ("Thousands of Inca Mummies Raised From their Graves"): "About 40 of the mummy bundles are topped with false heads, known to archaeologists as *falsas cabezas*. Such heads, some covered with wigs, were known to be attached to mummy bundles that encased members of the Inca elite. Until this discovery, only one *falsa cabeza* from the Inca period is believed to have been documented. Also recovered were 50,000 to 60,000 artifacts, from personal valuables to food and everyday utensils."

The discovery provides archaeologists and historians with evidence of how the Inca people lived, their burial rites, and beliefs.

A site in the Inca city of Armatambo has yielded hundreds of mummies and skeletons and given archaeologists like this one a detailed look at the life of the Incas.

The evidence is considered very reliable, since the mummy bundles lay undisturbed. The mummies were preserved under ideal conditions, and hair and skin remain intact.

The graveyard was found under an area where poor people live in shacks. It is named Tupac Amaru after the last Inca ruler. It provided a refuge for Andes residents who left the mountains during the 1980s to escape violence by local political groups.

Textile cooperatives (businesses run jointly by their members) in Ecuador and Peru keep up the ancient traditions of weaving and spinning and also provide Native peoples with income. Among the most successful weavers' cooperatives are those at Otavalo and Taquile. Otavalo weavers sell their textiles at a market in Quito, Ecuador. They produce tapestries, cloth, belts, blankets, and other goods using either the traditional backstrap looms of their Inca ancestors or larger treadle looms, similar to those brought to Ecuador by the Spanish. A treadle loom has wooden frames and a foot pedal, or treadle. Taquile, an island in Peru, has been home to a colony of weavers for centuries.

The colors and designs of Taquile textiles tell whether a man is married or single. A knitted cap with white tufts shows a man is available. Red peaks on a cap indicate he is married. Taquile belt designs depict seasonal or calendar events, such as the month for repairing roofs or planting crops.

Major Peruvian cities, such as Lima, Cuzco, and Arequipa, have become financial centers where industry, mining, and banking dominate. Yet the economy of the Inca region struggles and many of those who live in poverty are descendants of Inca subjects.

Peru is in a financial crisis, with more than half of the population living below the poverty line. Young *indígenas* leave their Andes villages to find work in the cities, but unemployment rates are around 9 percent. They find themselves living in shacks on the outskirts of the cities in conditions far worse than their home villages.

The economies of Ecuador and Colombia depend heavily on agriculture. They produce bananas, coca, and coffee for export, along with staple foods such as corn and potatoes. Nearly 40 percent of Ecuador's citizens live in poverty. Unemployment is more than 10 percent and inflation is now controlled at just over 3 percent. Nearly 50 percent of Colombia's citizens live in poverty, while a handful of Colombians rank among the wealthiest people in the world. Colombian unemployment stands at 11 percent.

Bolivia is the poorest country in South America. The economy depended on tin, accounting for nearly one-third of all exports. When tin prices dropped worldwide in 1985, the Bolivian economy collapsed. The loss of tin mining as a moneymaker has led to a rise in illegal coca farming. Today, coca and cocaine production accounts for half of the nation's exports and is a major problem. As in Ecuador, poverty strikes six out of 10 people in Bolivia.

Chile's citizens fare better than their neighbors. Chileans earn more per person than most other South Americans. Industry and service jobs comprise three-fourths of the jobs filled by the Chilean labor force. Although unemployment hovers at 8 percent, inflation is low and consumer goods are readily available.

Yale and Peru Reach a Settlement

When archaeologists from Yale University uncovered the ancient Inca cities of Cuzco and Machu Picchu, they took many artifacts back to the United States. For some time now, the government of Peru has wanted them back.

After several heated discussions, Yale and Peru reached an agreement in 2007. Peru will build a new museum and research center in Cuzco to display the Inca artifacts. Yale will recognize Peru's ownership of objects found in university digs, such as bones and other artifacts from Machu Picchu. The two parties will continue Inca research as a joint project.

Most of the materials in question were collected by Hiram Bingham beginning in 1911. Peru claimed that while Bingham was given permission to study the artifacts he found, he was never told he could keep them. The agreement resolves the dispute to the satisfaction of both parties.

Conservation and environmental issues concern Andes residents, many of whom live in tune with the natural world. In Peru, uncontacted cultures (tribes that have no contact with the outside world) face invasion by loggers determined to illegally collect mahogany trees from protected lands. These lands belong to the tribes who live on them, such as the Amahuacas, the Shanamahuas, and the Yora Yaminaguas, and the tribes have met the arrival of logging teams with bows and arrows. They also string thick vines across rivers to prevent access to their land by boats. Although the harvest of mahogany in this region is illegal, stolen wood can yield the thieves millions of dollars each year.

Pollution from mining operations, air pollution in cities, cutting down forests, and water pollution are some of the environmental problems faced by peoples of the region today. In Ecuador, Peru, and northern Chile, deserts are expanding. This adds to soil erosion and reduces productivity in villages where farming remains the mainstay of the people. Environmental problems are caused by sprawling cities, industrialization, and increased population, and affect all citizens. Each of the countries has developed federal conservation plans. Their success remains to be seen.

After 800 years, the basic structures that once supported the Inca Empire survive. Traces of roads, agricultural terraces, and irrigation ditches carve their patterns across the land. Remains of architecture, artistry, and religion endure despite efforts to erase them from history.

Quechua, the language of the people, is still spoken today. The Inca lifestyle and commitment to community living continues in Quechua families. The Inca work ethic flourishes in the warp and weft of back-strap looms. Their shuttles carry homespun yarns to produce textiles of remarkable beauty that are a living legacy of their ancestors.

TIME LINE

ca. 1200	Manco Capac and Mama Ocllo found the Inca Empire and the city of Cuzco.
1228–1258	Sinchi Roca, Manco Capac's heir, builds agricultural terraces and drains the local marsh near Cuzco, ensuring an adequate food supply for the growing empire.
1258–1288	Lloque Yupanqui improves the Intihuasi and builds the Acllahuasi, creates public markets, begins building the extensive Inca road system, and establishes the Inca administrative system.
1288–1318	Mayta Capac establishes a school system among Inca nobility, encourages religious tolerance, and conquers the people of Tiahuanaco, a culture of superb builders and masons.
1318–1348	Capac Yupanqui rebuilds the Intihuasi and Acllahuasi and extends the empire westward to the Pacific Ocean.
1348–1378	Inca Roca reorganizes the Inca political and social structure.
1438–1471	Cusi Yupanqui defeats the Chanca and proclaims himself Sapa Inca, taking the name Pachacuti. He rebuilds Cuzco. He and his son and grandson greatly expand the empire.
1493–1525	Huayna Capac extends the empire into present-day Ecuador and Colombia, and declares Quito a second capital.
1525	Huayna Capac dies of smallpox. Civil war divides the empire.
1532	Francisco Pizarro, the Spanish conquistador, captures Atahuallpa.
1533	Atahuallpa is tried and executed by the Spanish.
1535	The Spanish make Manco Inca the leader of the empire, but he has no power. Pizarro's younger brother, Gonzalo, takes charge in Cuzco, sparking an Inca rebellion. Manco Inca flees.
1544	Manco Inca is murdered by followers of Diego de Almagro, Pizarro's business partner.
1572	The Spanish execute Tupac Amaru, the last true Sapa Inca. The last outpost of the Inca Empire, Vilcabamba, falls into ruin.
1911	Archaeologist Hiram Bingham rediscovers the hidden city of Machu Picchu.
2002	Thousands of Inca mummies are discovered outside Lima, Peru.
2007	Yale University and the government of Peru agree that they will jointly study the ancient Inca cities of Cuzco and Machu Picchu. Inca artifacts in Yale's museum will be returned to Peru.

GLOSSARY

acllas holy or chosen women

adobe bricks made of straw and mud and dried in the sun

alloy a blend of various metals

anthropologist a person who studies human societies

anthropomorphize to give animals human forms or personality

apu regional head

aqueduct an artificial channel for carrying water

architect a person who designs buildings

artifact an object made by a person, usually something left behind by a past culture

assimilate to absorb and integrate people and ideas into a wider culture

ayllu clan

barter to trade goods or services for items considered by both parties to be of equal value

bola a weapon made of a rope with three stones attached

Capac Incas people who were born into the nobility

caravan a group of people traveling together, often traders

chicha corn-based beer

citadel a high fortress

clan a group of close-knit families

coya primary wife of the Sapa Inca

cronista Spanish soldiers, clerks, and priests who wrote detailed accounts of the history, customs, and daily lives of Inca citizens

curaca a professional Inca government employee

Hahua Incas appointed nobles

heathen someone who does not believe in Christianity

huaca shrine or sacred place

idol an image of a god

irrigation bringing water to the fields to help crops grow

lance a weapon with a hard point mounted on a wooden pole

litter a small carriage carried by several men

mace a heavy club with a metal head studded with spikes

mason a person who works or builds with stone or brick

masonry stonework

missionary someone sent to promote his or her religion in a foreign country

mitima resettlement; when an entire village or sections of that village were forcibly moved from their home to new, pro-Inca locations

mortar the cement used to bond together bricks or stones in building

mosaic pictures made with pieces of colored tile

mural wall painting

myth a traditional story, often with a magical element

omen a sign or event that foretells the future

oral history remembering history by telling stories

pagan a person who is not a Christian

polygamy having more than one wife

polytheism worshipping more than one god

quinoa a type of grain that is native to the Andes Mountains

quipu the Inca knot database, used to record population, crop and manufacturing yields, and assess taxes

Sapa Inca the supreme ruler of the Inca Empire

scribe a person who copies out documents

succession passing on the family's rank

terracing building a number of flat platforms, usually into the side of a hill; terrace farming is farming the land that is on these flat platforms

textiles cloth, or the items made from cloth

tunic a loose garment that usually reached to the wearer's knees

urn a tall, rounded vase

BIBLIOGRAPHY

Ascher, Marcia, and Robert Ascher, *Mathematics of the Incas: Code of the Quipu*. Mineola, N.Y.: Dover Publications, 1981.

Bernand, Carmen, *The Incas: People of the Sun*. New York: Harry N. Abrams, 1993.

de Betanzos, Juan, *Narrative of the Incas* (*Suma y narracíon de los Incas*). Translated by Roland Hamilton and Dana Buchanan. Austin, Tex.: University of Texas Press, 1996.

Bierhorst, John, *Black Rainbow*. New York: Farrar, Strauss and Giroux, 1976.

Bordewich, Fergus M, "Winter Palace," Smithsonian. com. Available online. URL: http://www.smithsonianmag.com/travel/winter.html. Accessed December 18, 2008.

Braun, David, "Thousands of Inca Mummies Raised From Their Graves," National Geographic News, April 22, 2002. Available online. URL: http://news.nationalgeographic.com/news/2002/04/0410_020417_incamummies.html. Accessed December 18, 2008.

Burger, Richard L. and Lucy C. Salazar, Ed., *Machu Picchu: Unveiling the Mystery of the Incas*. New Haven, Conn.: Yale University Press, 2004.

Callañaupa, Nilda, "A Message from Nilda Callañaupa," Descendants of the Incas. Available online. URL: www.incas.org/87.html. Accessed December 18, 2008.

Chuchiak IV, John F., Lecture #29, "Colonial Responses to the Bourbon Reforms: Discontent and Indian Rebellions in the Viceroyalties of Peru & New Spain (1748–1800)." Available online. URL: http://history.smsu.edu/jchuchiak/. Accessed April 23, 2003.

de Cieza de León, Pedro, *Chronicle of Peru* (The Second Part of the Chronicle of Peru). Translated by Clements R. Markham. London: Hakluyt Society, 1883.

Cobo, Father Bernabé, *The History of the New World*. Translated by Roland Hamilton. Austin, Tex.: University of Texas Press, 1983.

Guaman Poma de Ayala, Felipe, *La nueva crónica y buen gobierno*. Biblioteca Ayacucho, 1980.

Hemming, John, *Monuments of the Incas*. Boston: Little, Brown and Company, 1982.

Jacobs, James Q., "Tupac Amaru, The Life, Times and Execution of the Last Inca." Available online. URL: http://www.jqjacobs.net/andes/tupac_amaru.html. Accessed December 18, 2008.

James, Peter, and Nick Thorpe, *Ancient Inventions*. New York: Ballantine Books, 1995.

Jaschik, Scott, "Yale and Peru Reach Pact on Artifacts," *Inside Higher Education*. Available online. URL: http://www.insidehighered.com/news/2007/09/17/yale. Accessed December 18, 2008.

Karen, Ruth, *Kingdom of the Sun*. New York: Four Winds Press, 1975.

Malpass, Michael, *Daily Life in the Inca Empire*. Westport, Conn.: Greenwood Publishing, 1996.

Marrin, Albert, *Inca and Spaniard: Pizarro and the Conquest of Peru*. New York: Macmillan Publishing Company, 1989.

Maugh, Thomas H., II. "Americas' Earliest Observatory Unearthed," *Los Angeles Times*, May 15, 2006.

de Molina, Cristóbal, *The Fables and Rites of the Incas*. Madrid, Spain: Historia 16, 1989.

"Palacio de la Conquista." The University of New Mexico Conexiones. Available online. URL: http://www.unm.edu/~conspain/trujillo/Palacio%20de%20la%20Conquista.html. Accessed December 18, 2008.

Pizarro, Pedro, *Relation of the Discovery and Conquest of the Kingdoms of Peru*. Translated by Philip Ainsworth Means. New York: Cortes Society, 1921.

Roach, John, "Machu Picchu Under Threat from Pressures of Tourism," National Geographic News, April 15, 2002. Available online. URL: http://news.nationalgeographic.com/news/2002/04/0415_020415_machu.html. Accessed December 18, 2008.

Sarmiento De Gamboa, Pedro, *History of the Incas*. Mineola, N.Y.: Dover Publications, 1999.

Stierlin, Henri, *Art of the Incas*. New York: Rizzoli International Publications, 1984.

Editors of Time Life Books, *Incas: Lords of Gold and Glory*. New York: Time Life Books, 1992.

"Tupac Amaru II." Incaita. Available online. URL: http://www.fortunecity.com/millennium/lilac/3/tupac.htm. Accessed December 18, 2008.

Urton, Gary, *Inca Myths*. Austin, Tex.: University of Texas Press, 1999.

de la Vega, Garcilaso, *The Incas: The Royal Commentaries of the Inca Garcilaso de la Vega*. Translated by Maria Jolas from the critical, annotated edition of Alain Gheerbrant. New York: The Orion Press, 1961.

Wilford, John Noble, "Incas scaled deep gorges with fiber bridges," International Herald Tribune. Available online. URL: http://www.iht.com/articles/2007/05/09/arts/snincas.php. Accessed December 18, 2008.

de Xeres, Francisco, *The Conquest of Peru (1534)*. Translated by Clements R. Markham. London: Hakluyt Society, 1970.

Zuidema, Reiner Tom, *Inca Civilization in Cuzco*. Austin, Tex.: University of Texas Press, 1990.

FURTHER RESOURCES

BOOKS

Clarke, Barry, and Elizabeth Baquedano. *Aztec, Inca, and Maya.* (New York: DK Publishing, 2005)

Want more pictures? This entry in the popular reference series includes hundreds more photos of artwork and artifacts. It also includes two other major South American empires, which makes for interesting comparisons to the Inca.

D'Altroy, Terence. *The Incas (Peoples of America)* (Boston: Wiley-Blackwell, 2003)

A well-reviewed book for stronger readers, this book traces the entire history of the Andes region, focusing on the Inca. Dozens of maps show how the empire was formed and spread.

Jones, David. *The Illustrated History of the Incas* (Boston: Southwater Publishing, 2008)

Hundreds of color photos of artwork, artifacts, archaeological digs, and paintings beautifully document the style and history of the Inca people.

Kaufman H.W. and J.E. *Fortifications of the Incas* (Botley, U.K.: Osprey Publishing, 2006)

Do you like forts and fortresses? This book is for you. It covers in detail the buildings of the Incas from the point of view of military defense. How did they build them? Why? Where can they be seen now? Read here to find out.

Malpass, Michael. *Daily Life in the Inca Empire* (Westport, Conn.: Greenwood Press, 1996)

Malpass explains in detail how the Incas lived, worked, prayed, and expanded their culture.

Sarmiento de Gamboa, Pedro. *History of the Incas* (Gloucester, U.K.: Dodo Press, 2007)

Not for every reader, but this book, translated from the original Spanish, is an interesting look by a 16th-century explorer at what the Spanish expeditions found on their journeys among the Incas. It includes many details about everyday life in the Inca Empire.

Thomson, Hugh. *The White Rock: An Exploration of the Inca Heartland* (New York: The Overlook Press, 2003)

This is the ideal book for people who would like to trek the Inca Trail through the Andes but do not have the money or energy. Thomson describes his own adventures in the Andes in vivid detail.

WEB SITES

Andes Manca
http://andesmanta.com/

Listen to the members of the Andes Manca quartet play authentic Andean music. These four brothers believe reviving the music can help bridge the gap between the Inca Empire and modern society.

Geometry Step by Step from the Incas
http://Agutie.homestead.com

Math lovers will find this site an ideal way to learn more about Inca science and history. Included in this site are dramatic views of Machu Picchu, with its walls and trapezoid-shaped doorways.

Hos-McGrane Projects: Inca Empire
www.internet-at-work.com/hos_mcGrane/inca/eg_inca_menu1.html

Take a look at the everyday life of the Incas, including what they wore and how they made clothes, the unwritten records of the quipus, agriculture, and crime and punishment. This is a comprehensive site, is easy to read, and is thorough.

Ice Treasures of the Incas

www.nationalgeographic.com/features/96/mummy/

The mummy of the Ice Maiden, discovered by archaeologists in 1995, renewed interest in the Inca people. This Web site enables you to travel along with the expedition.

Inca Civilization

http://Coe.fgcu.edu/students/webb/meso/inca.htm

The opening of this site provides a map of South America and a closer view of the Inca empire. The text discusses culture, religion, recreation, daily life, and food. The site has activities for people interested in getting a better understanding of Inca life.

Inca: A Virtual Exhibit

www.mnsu.edu/edmuseum/prehistory/latinamerica/south/cultures/inca.html

This is an online exhibit of the culture and technology of the Inca people. The site provides a map and photos of sites in Peru, as well as written text on Inca customs and architecture.

Inca Weaving

www.incas.org.pe/English

Weaving has been a way of life for Peruvian people since the days of the Incas. Discover how the women of the Center for Traditional Textiles of Cuzco keep their heritage alive.

The Incas of Peru

http://Incas.perucultural.org.pe/English/

An overview of the Inca Empire, including its history, how its was organized, and Inca technology. The site includes several maps, and a gallery showing Inca buildings and artifacts.

The Incredible Incas

www.incas.mrdonn.org/empire.html

Read legends about llamas, and the hero Pachacuti and other Sapa Incas. Designed for elementary students, this site offers everything needed for writing an interesting report about the Incas.

Nova Online: Ice Mummies of the Inca

www.pbs.org/wgbh/nova/peru/worlds/

High in the Andes, the Incas sacrificed young people and placed their bodies in burial sites. The cold climate mummified their bodies. Recently, archaeologists discovered some of these bodies. Read about their stories here.

Primary Source: Chronicles of the Incas, 1540

www.fordham.edu/halsall/mod/1540cieza.html

Read the chronicles of Pedro de Cieza de Léon, a Spanish conquistador. This journal, written in 1540, gives the eyewitness views of a conqueror about the Inca people.

PICTURE CREDITS

INDEX

Note: **Boldface** page numbers indicate
  major discussions of topics; *italic*
  page numbers indicate illustra-
  tions; page numbers followed by *c*
  indicate chronology entries; page
  numbers followed by *g* indicate
  glossary entries; page numbers
  followed by *m* indicate maps.

ABOUT THE AUTHOR

BARBARA A. SOMERVILL is a professional children's nonfiction writer with more than 150 published books. She is the author of *Electrical Circuits*, *Plant Reproduction*, and several works on recovering animal species, and, under the pseudonym Sophie Lockwood, a series on insects and another on mammals. Somervill is a member of the Society of Children's Book Writers and Illustrators and the North Carolina Writer's Network.

Historical consultant LUCY C. SALAZAR, PH.D., specializes in Inca archaeology and the early prehistory of Peru. She is co-curator of the Machu Picchu exhibition and curatorial affiliate in anthropology at Yale University's Peabody Museum, and coauthor of *Machu Picchu: Unveiling the Mystery of the Incas*.